Dear President Obama

Published in the United States by
Beckham Publications Group, Inc.
P.O. Box 4066, Silver Spring, MD 20914

ISBN: 978-0-9823876-1-0
0-9823876-1-X
Library of Congress Control Number: 0-9823876-1-X

Linda Ellerbee photograph by Rolfe Tessem
Bruce Kluger photograph by Sarina Finklestein
David Tabatsky photograph by Kai Heinrich

Dear President Obama

Letters of Hope from Children Across America

Bruce Kluger and David Tabatsky

Foreword By Linda Ellerbee

Silver Spring

Change
Change

FOREWORD

AS A PRODUCER AND HOST of *Nick News*, a documentary series for children that airs on Nickelodeon, I am in my 19th year of listening to kids speak about school, divorce, abuse, love, hate, racism, honor, religion, courage, life, and, yes, death. I've listened to their thoughts about wars, terrorism, politics, the environment and the behavior of nations. Most of all, I've listened to their hopes and dreams. And still the most common reaction I get from "grownups" when they watch one of our shows is, "But these kids are so smart!" This is almost always said with surprise if not downright shock.

The truth is, they are smart. And frighteningly honest. When Senators Barack Obama and John McCain sat down with us to answer kids' questions, most of the questions were about familiar issues and evoked familiar answers. But then one kid said, "Hello, my name is Kedric and I'm 13, and I know what it feels like to be picked last for the football team at school. I was wondering, have you ever been picked last and how did you handle it?"

The answers the two men gave to that question revealed more about them, more about who they are and what they're made of, than we saw in any of the "grownup" debates. But it took a kid to ask the question.

And that is the kind of honesty you will find in this book.

You see, kids get it. They really get it. And, after getting it, they often want to change it. They believe they can change their world. They believe they will. They understand that citizenship doesn't start when you're 18; it starts the day you're born. They are passionate and they want to participate. Never have we at *Nick News* seen this more clearly than in the presidential campaign of 2008 followed by the election of Barack Obama. I leave it to experts to explain why this particular campaign, this election, caught fire with the children of America. I know only that it did. For instance, here are the kinds of sentiments we heard from kids over and over, across the country, in cities and in small towns:

Said Lara, "It sort of feels like it's a new dawn." Said Christian: "On Election Day, I got to pull the lever. To me it felt like I was like actually a part of the change." Said Olivia: "It's just kind of magical!"

Magical? Yes, I believe it was. Call it the American magic.

Certainly race played a part in the excitement. More to the point, races played a part. It took Americans of all colors and backgrounds coming together to elect a man who is both black and white, a man who has referred to himself as a "mutt." I like that. In this country, in the end, we are all mutts. And we ought to be proud of it. I know we like to talk about the idea of "color-blindness," but in doing so, I think we miss the point. What if, instead, we worked at embracing each other's diversity? Celebrating our differences. We know that inside we are all more alike than we are different, but our differences count, too. They matter. Especially when, rather than denying them or trying to erase them, we allow them bring us together.

When I was young, there was a song called "We Shall Not Be Moved." It was often sung during the civil rights movement because it was about strength and courage. The song had many verses. One of them said, "Black and white together, we shall not be moved." What it really meant was that, together, we cannot be stopped.

Reading these letters to President Obama, I consider what wonders we may see if the kids of today can hang onto this passion, this hope, this wanting to do the right thing; if they can come together to make change for the good, to fight for justice, and to never, ever stop caring about their country, its citizens and our beautiful, spectacular, inspiring, all-American differences. After all, as President Obama said, "There is not a black America and white America and Latino America and Asian America. There is the United States of America."

And here are the kids to prove him right. Pay attention to their letters. They are the future speaking to us.

Linda Ellerbee
February 2009

ACKNOWLEDGMENTS

The creation of this book would not have been possible without the support and assistance of countless friends, relatives and educators from across the country. We would like to thank the following people for their enthusiastic participation in *Dear President Obama*:

The teachers, principals, administrators and students at: Braeside School, Highland Park, Illinois; Clinton Elementary School, Lincoln, Nebraska; Cooper Middle School, McLean, Virginia; Hongwanji Mission School, Honolulu, Hawaii; Indian Woods Middle School, Shawnee Mission, Kansas; Roosevelt Public School, Roosevelt, New Jersey; Trailridge Middle School, Lenexa, Kansas; Ulloa Elementary School, San Francisco, California; Urbana Middle School, Ijamsville, Maryland; Watchung Elementary School, Montclair, New Jersey

Our heartfelt thanks also go to Brian DeFiore, Linda Ellerbee, Barry Beckham, Marlo Thomas & Phil Donahue, Alene Hokenstad, Sara Dillon and Daniel Neiden for their dedicated support and guidance throughout this book's evolution.

Additional gratitude to: Jennifer Lawry Adams, Willie Banks, Diane Baxley, Rosalinde Block, Alan Bomser, Emily Braman & Alan Sickling, Leigh & Kara Carter, Niffer Clarke & Jonathan Levine, Rebecca Cohen, Holly Eardley, Lindsay Farrell, Tim & Terri Foley, Carol Fong, Donald Francis, Paul Gilbert, Bert Goolsby, Beth Greer, Phyllis Halliday, Larry Hiler, Nancy Hobson, Marta & Laura Hokenstad, Trisha Hoppmann, Teri Keeton, Lisa Kennedy, Betsy Kirchner, Patricia Kritzman, Kathy Lawry, Dan Levine, Jay Levy & Kerry Ann McCarthy, Donald Liebenson, Lucky Duck Productions, Mona Manley, Buzz McClain, Kyle Nakamoto, Assenka Oksiloff, Mary Jo Pagano & Marty Toub, Shari Payson, Arlene Randall, Kathi Reifschneider, Dr. Carol Riley, Jean Roberts, Geralyn Ruane, Laurie Rubin, Susan Schram, Bernie Shapiro, David Slavin, Cari Taira, Maralyn Tabatsky, Anthony Terrell, Jo Theis, Diane Tobin & Reed Donahue, Frank Vetter, Steven & Nina Wernick, Wendy Whidden...and to Stella Lemper Tabatsky, whose November 2008 letter to President-elect Barack Obama (pg. 5) was the inspiration for this book.

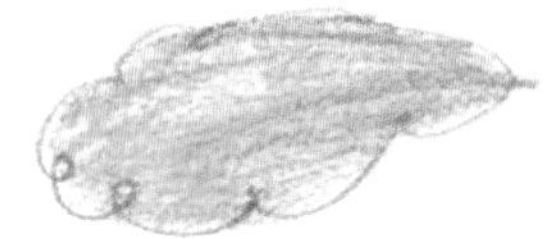

INTRODUCTION

"It is easier to build strong children than to repair broken men."
— Abolitionist Frederick Douglass, 1864

LIKE MOST SEISMIC EVENTS, Barack Obama's ascendancy to the American presidency meant different things to different people. To his party faithful, it was the long-awaited changing of the guard, a transformation of the political landscape orchestrated by a man possessed of a measured and hopeful vision for the future. To political historians, it was an unprecedented triumph by the most unlikely of candidates—young, unknown, itinerant—that captured the imagination of a nation torn by anxiety. And to Americans of a certain age, it was the most unfathomable event of their lifetimes: the repudiation of the very racism that had stained this country's proud claim to freedom since before its founding.

To children, however, the election of Barack Obama as America's 44th President was something less nuanced. Raised in an era of media saturation, kids today were more likely to view the 2008 election through the prism of modern-day reality shows: In the end, the best guy won for the obvious reasons—he was cool, he was smart, he was good looking, and he sure knew how to play the crowds.

And yet…there was something else. Today's children came of age during the sleepy prosperity of the nineties and the tense passion play that sprung from the rubble of September 11th. And while both Bill Clinton and George W. Bush inarguably had their shining moments of command during their presidencies, neither man seemed to electrify the electorate in quite the same way as the 47-year-old, mixed-race, Hawaii-born community organizer from Chicago.

Why was this? Current events played a large part. For the first time since the 1930s, America is suffering multiple ruptures in its foundation, from the economic meltdown at home, to two wars abroad, to the looming environmental crisis. It is no accident that the Obama campaign found success in its clarion call for sweeping change. In times of desperation, America has always exhibited an uncanny fearlessness about going back to the drawing board. The 2008 election proved no exception.

Then there was the oratory. Throughout his 21-month campaign, Barack Obama galvanized Americans by daring them not just to ponder the possible, but to dream the impossible; and he did so with words that spilled beyond the frame of the teleprompter and into the hearts of a nation hungry for inspiration. Although his rivals often tried to challenge the authenticity of his oratorical gifts, Barack Obama's eloquent enunciation of an "audacity of hope" was something rare and special in presidential politics.

And so the idea behind *Dear President Obama* was a relatively simple one: to recapture the exhilarating spirit of the 2008 election from the perspective of our nation's youngest citizens.

The day after the election, we began emailing a select handful of friends and relatives, asking them if their children would like to write a letter to the President-elect. Eager to test the waters, but unsure of the response we'd get, we kept our outreach modest. To our surprise—and delight—the children and parents we'd contacted not only responded positively, but launched an unexpected grass-roots effort of their own, forwarding our email to their relatives and friends, in the end reflecting the same kind of infectious enthusiasm that fueled the Obama campaign itself.

The final product is in these pages: In nearly 200 letters and drawings from every region of the country—from the seventh-grader in a Manhattan private school, to the nine-year-old in one of the poorest schools in Nebraska—these children, ages 4 through 18, do what kids do best: enunciate their hopes, fears and dreams about the world they live in, and their unchecked excitement about the historic election that took place during their young lives.

Naturally, in many of letters (which were written after the election, but before the inauguration) the children express observations they'd obviously gleaned from the grown-ups in their lives—their parents, their teachers, their family members. And yet the way in which they re-frame the news is all kid, especially when they discuss the environment.

"I want my children's children to see polar bears!" writes ten-year-old New Yorker Paola Wernick.

"How are you going to make this continent greener?" asks Claire Mortenson, 11, of Utah.

And more than a few of the children accompany their letters with colorful, hopeful drawings of our planet, floating serenely in space.

The tone of the letters is frequently warm and familiar. "I feel like if I knew you," writes third-grader Emily Bloomfield, "I could trust you like I trust a friend. "One of the children even assumes that the 44th president knows him.

"Dear President Obama," begins eight-year-old Isaac Pagano-Toub, "I am the kid who sent you $4.74 during the campaign..."

Not surprisingly, many of the children broach the issue of race in their letters, acknowledging Barack Obama's historical crossing of the color line with both awe and pride. For a few of the kids, their words are at once hopeful and heart-breaking.

"I was happy to see that someone who looks like me can be President of the United States of America," writes Casey Mack, 14, of Connecticut. "The kids at school have been saying some mean things about people who look like us. But now I believe we can change their negative points of view."

In February of 2008, musician will.i.am created a music video that quickly became emblematic of the heart of the Obama campaign. Adapted from candidate Obama's startlingly optimistic concession speech after the New Hampshire primary, the song, "Yes We Can," became an instant viral hit on the internet, and ultimately cemented the Obama campaign's three-word slogan. It was will.i.am's hope that the song would inspire children everywhere to memorize the uplifting speech, and in the process, apply those words to their lives.

Similarly, we hope that the voices of the children in this book will help set the tone for the remarkable journey on which America is now embarking.

Bruce David

Bruce Kluger and David Tabatsky
March 2009

DRAWING BY EMILIO ZUNIGA, 9, LINCOLN, NEBRASKA

Election Night in My House

Hannah Levine, 12 Years Old
New York, New York

The night drags on and on and on. History is waiting to be made, and we are waiting, too. What results will tonight bring? Four years of salvation or four of the same old? Who will sleep in peace tonight and who will toss and turn?

Every now and then, good news-bad news pops up on the television. Every hour or so, new states come in to play; more and more citizens are added to the mix.

And we wait.

Dad sprawled out on the couch, watching intently, almost wishing he could just go to bed, but not wanting to miss this. Mom sitting erect in the old blue chair staring at the screen. Me laying in my bean bag, sleepy but refusing to sleep. The night drags on, but that's not to say it's not interesting! There are many surprises coming up throughout the evening. Virginia…Florida…Ohio!

Things are looking very, very good. Our moods lift, lift, lift—spirits soaring unimaginable distances as we realize the future of our nation is to be almost inevitably superb.

At last, the reporters say that yes, a projection can be made. *His* face comes up on the screen, a giant yellow checkmark next to his name. A collective gasp from my family. I swear, I even heard the cat suck in a sharp breath as my head tilts back, arms raised to the sky in thanks. Mom is on her feet already, staring at the screen in disbelief and sheer joy. I join her, and we hold each other, there in the middle of the living room. I feel her shudder in my arms; she sniffles a bit in my ear.

A shudder, a sniff, and a smile, and history has been made.

The Letters

CAMILLE SULLIVAN, 8, LINCOLN, NEBRASKA

> "Tonight, we gather to affirm the greatness of our nation, not because of the height of our skyscrapers, or the power of our military, or the size of our economy. Our pride is based on a very simple premise, summed up in a declaration made over two hundred years ago."
> —Barack Obama

DEAR PRESIDENT
OBAMA.
HELP SCHOOLS
WHENEVER
YOU CAN. HOW OLD
ARE YOU? I AM 4.
FROM,
JACK
ADAMS

JACK ADAMS, 4, SHAKER HEIGHTS, OHIO

From the desk of *MITCH HALLIDAY*

Dear Mr. President,

You talked about changing America—well, here's something I would like changed. Everyone thinks America should solve all the problems in the world, and everyone asks the U.S. for help. Americans donate money to starving children around the world, but what about the adults and children at home? They don't get publicity, and they go unnoticed. We have social programs, but most are inadequate—like here in the northwest. There are shelters that fill up every night, and some people are left outside. Same thing with our "tent cities," most of which have their residents evicted.

You talked about change, and this is a problem that requires the utmost concern and action. Before we go about saving the world, we need to solve our own problems at home. Do you plan to reform the current programs without raising taxes—because it seems like we spend constantly with no change at all?

Thanks,
Mitch Halliday

MITCH HALLIDAY, 18, BELLEVUE, WASHINGTON

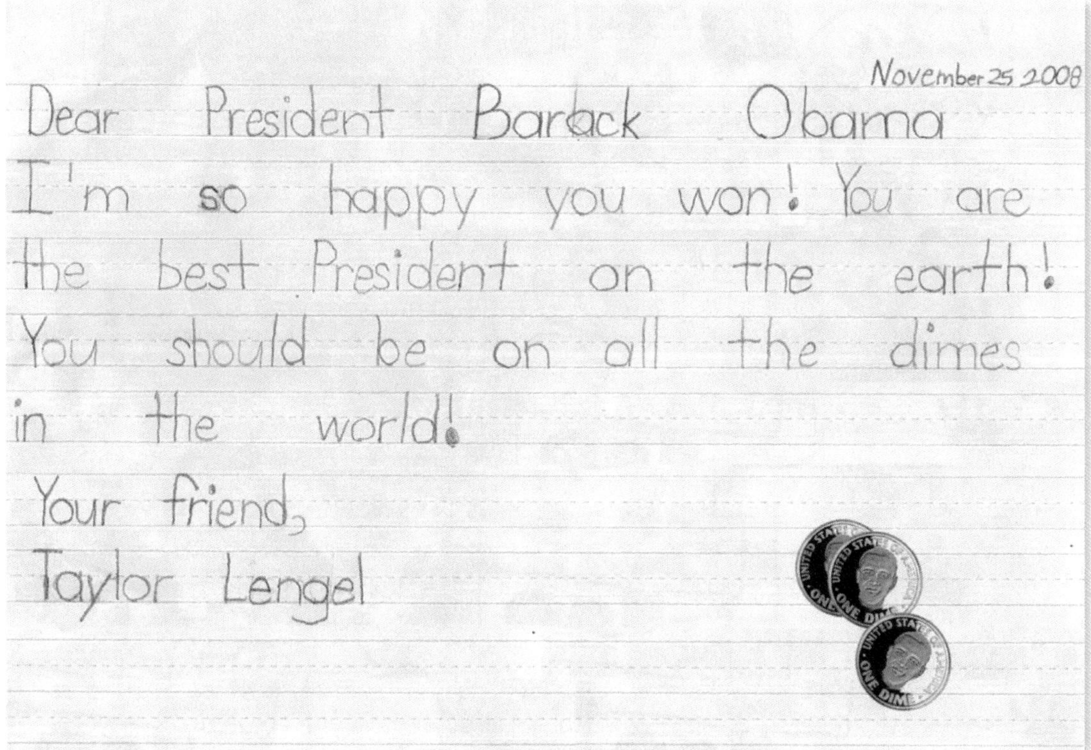

November 25 2008

Dear President Barack Obama
I'm so happy you won! You are the best President on the earth! You should be on all the dimes in the world!

Your friend,
Taylor Lengel

TAYLOR LENGEL, 7, LINCOLN, NEBRASKA

CASEY MACK

November 24, 2008

Dear Mr. Barack Obama,

You being president made me feel very excited. I was happy to see that someone who looks like me can be President of the United States of America. I have had some hard times at my school during the election. The kids have been saying some mean things about people who look like us. I tried talking to the students -- it did not work. So I went to my teachers who helped me find a solution. When I listened to your incredible speech and heard you say, "Yes We Can!" I started to believe we can change the student's negative points of view at school.

There is another reason why I am so excited that you will be president. You see, my brother and I are very sick. My brother has brain tumors and I have two rare disorders. My Mom has been worried all these years that we would not get health insurance because of our terrible sickness. If my brother does not have health insurance he would not get his medicine and he would die. My Mom moved us from Florida to Connecticut so we could have health insurance. She wants us to have a good education, too. I really miss Florida because I miss my family and friends. However, I realize that it is better to have insurance. Maybe, someday we can have insurance and live anywhere we want to live. I believe this is possible because you are going to be president. As you said before, we do need change.

I believe it ....YES WE CAN!

Your friend,
Casey Mack
Trumbull, CT

P.S. I can vote for you in the next election!

CASEY MACK, 14, TRUMBULL, CONNECTICUT

Dear Barack Obama,

I am only twelve years old, but I am so honored to be alive to witness the history you have made. Our country needs you.

Recently, my dad volunteered for your campaign, knocking on doors in Pennsylvania. When he gave me this news, it just made me so excited and made me realize that this is really happening. I realized that you, Barack Obama, could be the President of the United States of America.

And now, you are. This is still sinking in for me, I can't imagine what it must be like for you. As much as you probably are excited and happy, I guess you're probably nervous about this huge responsibility that you are taking on. I mean really, you're President!

I will do everything I can, and I hope that everyone will do everything they can to help you make this country a better, safer and happier place.

You are definitely our nation's ideal president-elect. You will, and you can, save this country—our country.

As you have said - and we should keep on saying - "yes we can."

Thank you for reading this.

Sincerely,

Stella♡

P.S. I am deeply sorry about your grandmother. I lost my grandmother last year and I know how you must be feeling.

STELLA LEMPER TABATSKY, 12, NEW YORK, NEW YORK

December 4, 2008

Dear President Elect Obama,

My name is Damon Duchai and I'm 8 years old. I have a fear about turkeys on Thanksgiving. My fear is that only one turkey gets pardoned. I think you should pardon more turkeys. How about pardoning 5 or 6? Please pardon more turkeys.

PLEASE!

From,
Damon Duchai

DAMON DUCHAI, JR., 8, ROOSEVELT, NEW JERSEY

KATE

Dear Mr. President Obama,

When I was in fourth grade we were asked to pick one of our heroes, dress up like them, and deliver a speech as if we were that person. I chose Dr. Martin Luther King. I was the only student who chose a hero that was cross-gender and cross-racial. There were no kids of color in my class. I remember being a little embarrassed as I walked to the front of the classroom. But when I began my speech, I felt proud of what I was saying and was happy with my choice.

I am now 16 and even though I am not old enough to vote, when you were elected, I felt so proud to be an American. Your speech that night moved me in the same way I was moved when I first read Dr. Martin Luther King's "I have a dream" speech. You are my new hero, and I wanted you to know that.

With my deepest respect and admiration,

Kate McCarty
Rumson, NJ

KATE MCCARTY, 16, RUMSON, NEW JERSEY

Dear President Obama,

My name is Wyatt Tobin, and I live in Montclair, New Jersey. I wish you and John McCain both won because you both are so handsome.

I hear you are looking for a dog as a pet! I have three dogs, Izzy, Ella and Hoagie. Hoagie is a beagle. Don't get a beagle. They eat their own poop.

Your friend,

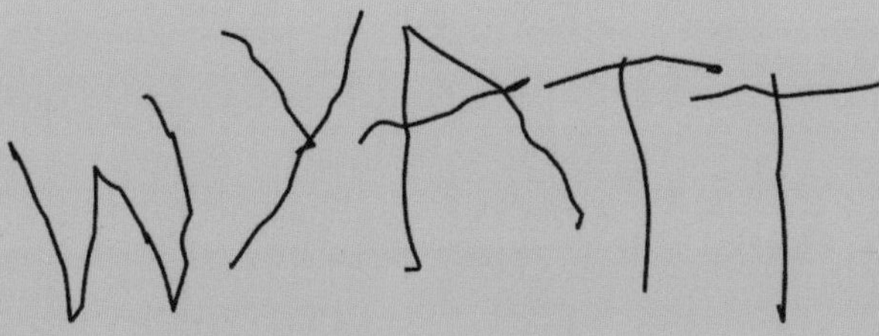

WYATT CLYDE TOBIN, 4, MONTCLAIR, NEW JERSEY

Date: Friday, January 2, 2009, 11:48 AM
From: Hannah Blockis
To: President-elect Barack Obama
Subject: Letter to Obama

Dear President Elect Obama,

I am a 13-year-old girl from New Hampshire and i am looking forward to a very bright future. I have my whole life planned out, from graduating high school, to going to Tufts University in Boston, to becoming a world famous veterinarian surgeon.

All of these dreams of mine could become quite expensive. One thing that will help would be lower taxes. I read that you and Mr. Biden would cut taxes 95% for working families. I think that is great! I also read that you are offering new tax benefits to help families like us to pay for college! That makes me very happy because really all i want to do in life is to graduate from Tufts University and become a great vetenary surgeon.

This letter to you, Mr. Obama, is about something i care about deeply, and i wanted you to know that you have a believer on your side and that i know you can do it!

Thank you so much for reading this. I am proud to be your citizen!

Your friend and citizen,
Hannah Blockis

Sent from my iPod

HANNAH BLOCKIS, 13, RYE, NEW HAMPSHIRE

Dear President Obama

Please Take care of The Homeless People and give Them food

Free The lions from The soo and send them to The moon.

Stop The war

-Juliet

JULIET BRUCE, 6, NEW YORK, NEW YORK

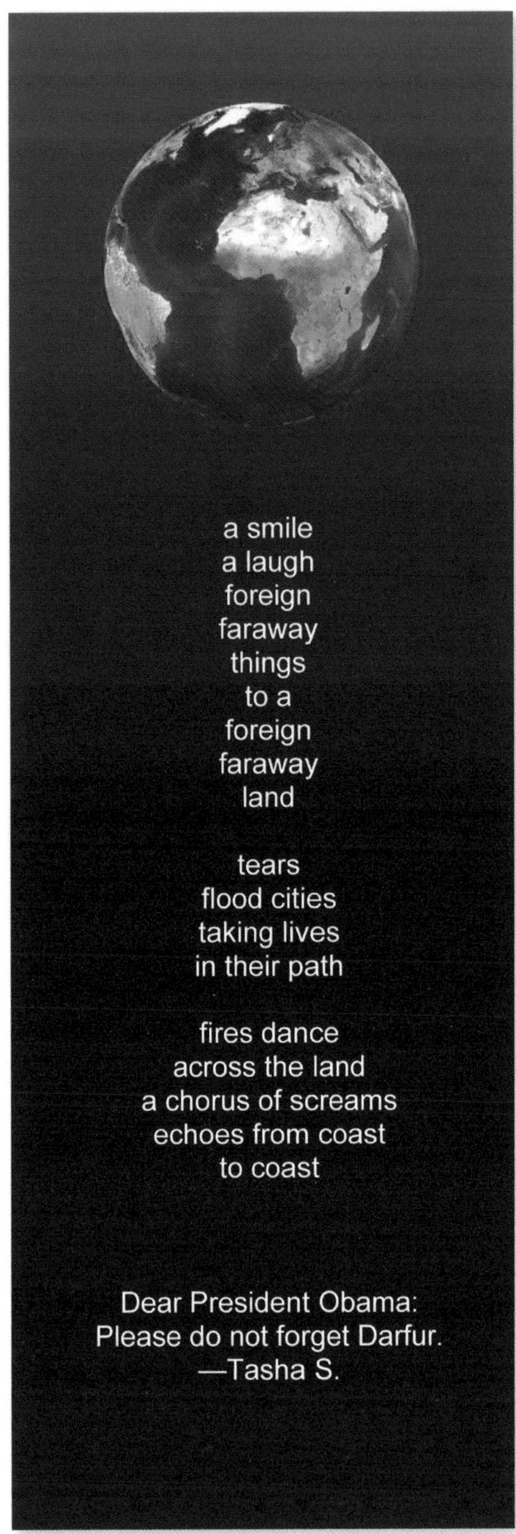

TASHA SLAVIN, 11, ST. LOUIS, MISSOURI

AMANTI DEBELO, 5, LINCOLN, NEBRASKA

"My parents shared not only an improbable love, they shared an abiding faith in the possibilities of this nation. They would give me an African name, Barack, or blessed, believing that in a tolerant America your name is no barrier to success."
—Barack Obama

These are some words of advice from Mr. Hiler's Second Grade class to President Obama, our 44th president.

Bring more jobs to our country.

Always remember that education is important for everyone.

Respect all opinions.

Accomplish world peace.

Consider banning guns.

Keep our environment pollution free and recycle more.

Obey "The Golden Rule".

Be the best that you can be.

Always take time to play basketball.

Make sure you read with your daughters.

Always make good health choices.

MR. HILLER'S SECOND GRADE CLASS, BRAESIDE ELEMENTARY SCHOOL, HIGHLAND PARK, ILLINOIS

Dear Mr. Obma, How old are you? I'm going to ask you another question. How many hats do you have? Can I have one of your hats? You are the best friend. Do you want to Know how many games I have? I hope you will do a good job of President. yep, how did you Know? I gest.
your friend
samir Al-Salimawi

SAMIR AL-SALIMAWI, 7, LINCOLN, NEBRASKA

December 5, 2008

Dear President Obama,
I am happy you are the President of the United States of America. I hope when you are President we won't have wars, guns, robbers and fighting. We will have world peace.

Sincerely,
Ryan Mack

RYAN MACK, 8, HIGHLAND PARK, ILLINOIS

November 26, 2008

Dear Barack Obama,

I am Larry Fulton. I am 11 years old and I live in Pepper Pike, Ohio.

Congratulations on winning the election. At first I doubted you would be frequently mentioned on the news, but as you quickly gained popularity, I knew you would win. I knew that change would come to America. Also, my middle school held a mini-election and you won by a landslide. After that, I knew you would win at least Ohio.

I, like you, am African-American. I'm happy you won because that sent a message to me and many other African-American people that you can do or be anything you want, regardless of your race.

During your campaign, you were an inspiration to me in the areas of politics and family. When your grandmother got sick, you went to visit her and didn't pretend like she wasn't so you could keep doing rallies to get votes. You took care of what was more important: family. Also, I always saw you with your wife and kids; John McCain, not so much. When there were debates, you were always the one who stayed calm and didn't focus your campaign on throwing insults at the other candidate. I also think your sensational speaking skills, in addition to your great ideas, helped you win.

Because of all these things, you greatly inspire me, and although it's not exactly my wish to be president some day, I really want to be like you.

Thank you for reading my letter, and I wish you good luck in the White House.

Sincerely,
Larry Fulton

LARRY FULTON, 11, PEPPER PIKE, OHIO

Dear Obama,

You are the first African American presedent. My brother Miles says that you are as nice as my Mama. Have a great day in office.

Love,
Theo

THEODORE COLBERT IV, 8, MONTCLAIR, NEW JERSEY

I WOULD LIKE A REAL CHIHUAHUA. AND THE SICK PEOPLE TO NOT GET SICK.

MADELINE

MADELINE SHERIDAN, 4, RESTON, VIRGINIA

Dear Barack Obama,

I'm a 13-year-old boy from Scranton, PA, and when I heard that there was a black candidate running for president, everyone around the country—including me—was shocked. But after a while, I wasn't shocked. I was glad.

Mr. Obama, you and I have a lot of things in common. Both of us have a white mother and a black father. You had a father who only saw you twice in your life before he died in a car crash in Kenya in 1982. My father wasn't really like that; and even though my parents argued at times—where my mom or my dad would move out—he was there for me. So I have it even a little better than you did.

But what we both have in common is that our mothers were always there for us, and our grandparents, too. All of this is important to me because, from your childhood until now, you have shown me that I could grow to be just like you, and to be able to accomplish things in life and make good things become better things.

So now we have you as President—a nice, intelligent man who the country hopes will defeat all odds and make America a better place for people all over the world. You showed everybody that the color of your skin doesn't matter; and what *does* matter is the good you can do for the people of the world, and the people of the United States.

I am really glad that you're President, Mr. Obama, and I hope that you do a good job.

Sincerely,
Jalen Parker

JALEN PARKER, 13, SCRANTON, PENNSYLVANIA

Dear presidentobaMa,

I am The Kid that Sent you $4.74.
you inspire Me to Do My HoMeWork in
The Morning. I Want you to Make
Better SchoolS. Can you Make less hunting animals?
You are a fintaskic New president.

Sincerely,

Isaac

Age 8

ISAAC PAGANO-TOUB, 8, NEW YORK, NEW YORK

From the desk of Moli Becker...

President Obama,

First of all let me tell you how much I love the fact that you won the Presidential election. I think you will do a great job--your ideas are great and wise.

America is my home. You see, I was adopted from China, and back them it wasn't as rich and successful a country as it is today and will continue to be. There are many people out there in the world who are still in orphanages, and my heart goes out to them. I know what it feels like to be abandoned and not taken care of. I feel so bad for them and hope that you will help them, now that you are president. I think that your first order of business should be either the economy, which is continuing to drop, or the war in Iraq. I think that pulling out the soldiers in Iraq is a great idea, but we should do it gradually. If we were to pull them all out at the same time, then there will be no protection at all, and we will be viewed as the bad guys.

I think that in order for America to prosper and continue to be a great nation, the president has to be able to relate to the people and their needs. They need to understand that sometimes power isn't always all that it's cracked up to be. In the words of Spiderman: "With great power, comes great responsibility." I think that he couldn't be any more right. America is the place that I have lived for the majority of my life. I have always loved living here and still do. America is my safe place, a place where I can be free and not be afraid. A place of never-ending possibilities. A place where there is no one who tells you who you should be, and what you should do, or what you should wear. A place where knowledge flows and never stops. A place where, no matter where you are, you can always feel at home.

America is where my heart is and it is where it shall always stay. And I know that it's where your heart is too. I think that with you as President America will not only rise to the top and be the best it can be, but it will also be looked upon as one of the greatest nations in the world, with you, Barack Obama, leading us to infinity and beyond.

Sincerely,
A passionate American citizen,
8th grader Moli Becker

MOLI BECKER, 13, MCLEAN, VIRGINIA

 Dear Obama, 

I am happy you have become president. I know you will help the economy, the environment, and all the other things that will help every country and every city in our state become one amazing community. I want you to turn our world from what we made it to what I, you, and everyone knows it should be. Think about the when the Native Americans found our land. It was clean, there was no polluting, but most important, when it was found it was a land of freedom. If everyone just stops to see what we have done to our world we could make a change. But we all have to stick together and all pitch in. I feel that helping our environment is not just saving animals, trees and our world, but it is saving you. I was also hoping you could try to stop racism because I think that if you are black or white, gay or strait, young or old, you are all connected in a way. I want this letter to be heard, to tell people what they are doing wrong, and what they riley truly need to do to help quickly.

Sincerely the girl who wants to make a change,

Audrey Rae Kluger

AUDREY KLUGER, 9, NEW YORK, NEW YORK

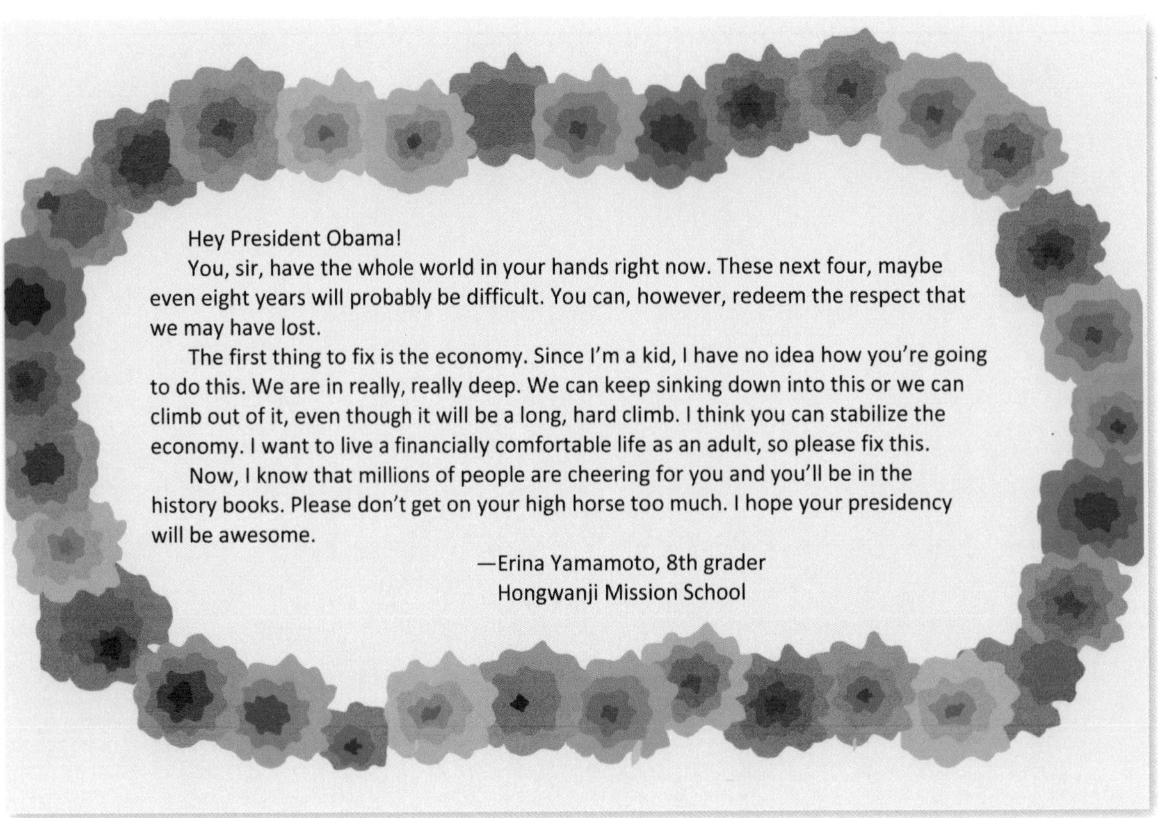

Hey President Obama!

You, sir, have the whole world in your hands right now. These next four, maybe even eight years will probably be difficult. You can, however, redeem the respect that we may have lost.

The first thing to fix is the economy. Since I'm a kid, I have no idea how you're going to do this. We are in really, really deep. We can keep sinking down into this or we can climb out of it, even though it will be a long, hard climb. I think you can stabilize the economy. I want to live a financially comfortable life as an adult, so please fix this.

Now, I know that millions of people are cheering for you and you'll be in the history books. Please don't get on your high horse too much. I hope your presidency will be awesome.

—Erina Yamamoto, 8th grader
Hongwanji Mission School

ERINA YAMAMOTO, 13, HONOLULU, HAWAII

Dear President Obama,

Congratulations on your win! I'm certain that you'll do a great job as the 44th president of the United States.

I may be only 10 years old, but I know that there are problems in the country that, as president, you should consider. Because what is wrong with America can change and become better. We will also show other countries how peace and solutions can work out.

In honor of your victory, I have written you an acrostic poem:

B—better America
A—amazing victory
R—raising the bar
A—always standing up for yourself
C—change is good
K—kids are important

O—outstanding speeches
B—big dreamer
A—afraid of nothing
M—modest
A—and way more

Enjoy your time at the White House. I know you will make us proud. Good luck!

Your Fellow American,
Samantha Abelson

SAMANTHA ABELSON, 10, MONTROSE, CALIFORNIA

INDIAN WOODS MIDDLE SCHOOL • SHAWNEE MISSION, KANSAS

"My grandma has sugar diabetes and it's getting worse. We had good memories, and I don't know how much time she has left. I would like you to look more into sugar diabetes." —Terrance Brockman, 12

Dear President Obama,

On April 16th 2007, thirty-three were left dead at the Virginia Tech Massacre. That day my friends and I were up at the school gym playing dodge ball against our parents. It was great fun, and after many rounds of the exhausting game we all ran out side, grabbed a popsicle and sat down to hang out. Everything was going jut fine until one of my best friends came over and told us what happened on the Virginia Tech campus.

"My cousin goes to Virginia Tech," he said, "and we can't get a hold of her."

Days later, my mom gave me the news. "Hey, Garrett, come here for a second, we need to talk." Then she told me that Ryan's cousin was one of the thirty-three. I sat there for a while, wondering what the family was going through.

Mr. Obama, students go to college to get an education, not for this. Thirty-three are dead. That is thirty-three too many. America needs your help.

Sincerely,
Garrett Mould

GARRETT MOULD, 12, OVERLAND PARK, KANSAS

"We need tighter gun control. Automatic rifles should not be available to the public. Hunting rifles are fine with me, but ten unarmed citizens are no match for one criminal with an automatic rifle. If we don't learn from the mistakes of our past we are doomed to repeat them." —Kyle Fairfax, 13

"Please, please help kids who do drugs, even if what they're doing is illegal. D.A.R.E. programs aren't enough." —Nick DeHaan, 12

"I have a cousin who had a good future ahead of him. He was doing everything right—until he was introduced to drugs. He made a wrong decision that put him in jail for a while. I would hate to see another family go what my family went through. As president, you should try to prevent drugs from entering the U.S." —Jawann Stennis, 13

"I think you should give social security to all immigrants who have been in U.S. for over 8 years and don't have a criminal record. My great aunt was sent back to her native country and is now she separated from her two daughters and husband. She is still trying to come back in the country." —Eddy Mortera, 13

"I used to have three grandpas when I was about eight or nine. My Grandpa Jeff is gone now. He died of leukemia, and I miss him so dearly. I ask of you one favor: try to find a cure for leukemia." —Cody Gibson, 12

"I think you should send more law enforcement to each city in the country. We need more police officers for our streets and houses, for our stores and malls, and also for our schools." —Andres Gomez, 12

"Even though you defiled segregation/ Don't have that define your administration.
The people need a leader who knows what to do/ Don't disappoint the ones who chose you."
—Rachel Franklin, 13

TRAILRIDGE MIDDLE SCHOOL • LENEXA, KANSAS

"Please stop the killing in Gaza. Babies and kids are getting killed, and I don't know anyone who can stop the madness but you. Muslims move to the U.S. because they don't want to die. My grandma and grandpa died in Gaza, and I can't do anything because I'm a kid. Please stop the killing in Gaza." —Waleed Saifan, 13

"You will be the president for the next four years while I am going to high school. Please try to lower taxes. Things are way too expensive for people trying to provide for their families. I expect you to be a great president and I know that you will not disappoint me." —Allie Soto, 14

"The U.S. economy isn't in very good shape. I hope the cost of college lessens so that people with low income can afford to get a good education." —Cecilia Smith, 13

"I am an eighth grader. War has been going on since I can remember; I think it should end. All troops should come home and be with their families. We should have peace again." —Kylie Skelton, 13

"Our country is in a falling economic state. I think we should have less government spending rather than $1.2 trillion more. The U.S. is no longer the most powerful country on Earth. You should try to stay on top of the wars, remain in control and disregard the manipulations from Russia." —Connor Kelley, 13

Trailridge Middle School

Dear President Obama:

I believe that you will help our economy return to the way it was when most people were getting by with a happy life and not stressing about money all the time. I hope that you will fix all of the problems. When I step into the world, I hope to see a better economy, less war on terror, and many other changes that this nation needs.

I want to be able to start a family and have a good life without worrying about money, and whether I can get on a plane safely or not. I think that you should pull troops out of that pointless war zone before the time we negotiated. I also think that you should try to lower the voting age so that I can be a part of re-electing you. I believe you will make a big difference in this nation fixing what mistakes others have made.

Sincerely,
Jeremy

JEREMY FARMER, 13, LENEXA, KANSAS

"I support your bravery and hope you can do good things for our country. We need a helping hand to guide us through this tough time. I hope that when I get out of school you have made choices and compromises to better our country. I really want to be able to survive on my own out in the world." —Nathan Rupp, 14

"I am very concerned with gas prices lately. I will be sixteen in two years and will probably be getting a vehicle, and I don't know how I am supposed to get the money to pay for the gas for it. Maybe while you're president, it might be possible for you to lower gas prices and fix the economy." —Tyler Jewell, 14

"I am a middle school student in the state of Kansas. I hope you do well in office and make our country a better place. I hope our country treats you good like you are treating us." —Nathan Brunner, 13

JASON PHAN, 5, LINCOLN, NEBRASKA

"We need to internalize this idea of excellence. Not many folks spend a lot of time trying to be excellent."
—Barack Obama

A LETTER TO PRESIDENT OBAMA, FROM MATTHEW, AGE 5
(as dictated to his Mom)

Dear Barack Obama:

I'm glad you won (but I think the election between you and John McCain should have been decided by a boxing match or basketball game). Here's what I want you to do as president:

1. You say you're going to stop the war, so I don't need to tell you to do that.
2. Tell the kids where there's war to move, so they don't get hurt.
3. If there are kids who can't get a hold of their cousins, you should help them.
4. Read books about not letting the animals out of the zoo.
5. Build secret weapons, and hide them on top of giant buildings.
6. Make every preschool have 3 stars.
7. Go swimming a lot.
8. Go on vacation in Japan, and go on the bullet train, like my friend Max, and make sure you stay three weeks. (My mother keeps asking me, "Why three weeks?" so I told her, "You'll just have to wait until he's President to find out!")
9. I have a dragon book that you could read to your kids. But you might not want to read out loud, because when you're President you have to talk a lot, like me. (But I don't actually talk a lot. It's just that people are always asking me questions all the time.)
10. Make taxes one dollar. Then Grandpa wouldn't get so mad.
11. Make Christmas come earlier.

Sincerely,

Matthew Kirchner
I'm 5 years old

MATTHEW KIRCHNER, 5, SHAKER HEIGHTS, OHIO

December 5, 2008

Dear President Obama,
I think we should stop killing tigers. Every July 2nd we should give money to the poor. We should give presents to children in the hospitals and children that are poor.

Your friend
Helene Bergmann

HELENE BERGMANN, 7, HIGHLAND PARK, ILLINOIS

25 Novemder 2008

Dear President Barack Odama,
I like you because you are a nice president. You are a beautiful President. You have a most beautiful wife and kids! My teachers name is Mr. Banks. He is a nice Teacher. My Friends like you too.
Your Friend,
Anthoney Nguyen

ANTHONY NGUYEN, 7, LINCOLN, NEBRASKA

ULLOA ELEMENTARY SCHOOL, SAN FRANCISCO, CALIFORNIA

"I think you make the gas prices go down, and you should stop the war because people are getting hurt fighting for our country. Also, I think you can let the police get more practice." —Justin Lee, 7

"Congratulations, Barack Obama! You are the boss of the United States. You will go to the White House with your wife and two daughters. You will take care of the earth. You will be the nice president. If an old man or old woman drops a pen or something, I think you will pick it up." —Tiffany Chang, 7

"I think our country needs more help in our money system. I think our environment is pretty good. I guess our troops are good enough. But we still need to improve." —Hender Lin, 7

"Please help raise the economy. Please help people get their jobs back. Please help save water. Please help people change their lives." —Devin Lee, 7

Dear President Elect Obama,
You have to focus on your job. You need to protect the earth. Congratulations! You did it! You are going to be the elected president. You also needed to focus on what youre doing. I think you should wear pretty clothes. You have to talk on the radio. Talk carefully on the radio and don't talk so fast because you're going to mess up when you talk too fast. Don't be nervous when you talk on the radio. You are going to go to the White House with your wife and your two daughturs. You are going to be the boss of the U.S.A. Are you suprised and happy that get to be a president? You will talk and exclaim what will you do to your team.
Sincerly,
Ashley Wu

ASHLEY WU, 8, SAN FRANCISCO, CALIFORNIA

"You can be a wonderful president if you try your best." — Nathaniel Janus Teng, 7

December 4, 2008

Dear President-elect Obama,

I am a 13-year-old 8th grader in Frederick, MD, and a student at Urbana Middle School. I am very happy to learn that you have decided to listen to the opinions of kids our age! I have some ideas about what you should work on as president.

The first thing that I would like to say is to help the environment. The air, the water, the trees, and the animals...what would the world be without them? I believe that you should help encourage people to protect them. What would the world be with out a healthy and clean environment?

I would also want to say to use more alternative sources of energy. It's a lot healthier for our planet, and can save us a lot of time, money and resources. It is also healthier for the environment. We could use alternative energies to make heat, using the sun, even in the winter; and electricity, using the wind. I know that we already have these things, but I feel that we should have more.

I know I probably sound like a environment loving, tree hugger right now. But I would just like to say, thank you so much for listening to my opinion. My best wishes to you as President of the United States of America.

Sincerely,

Emily Mitnick

Emily Mitnick

EMILY MITNICK, 13, FREDERICK, MARYLAND

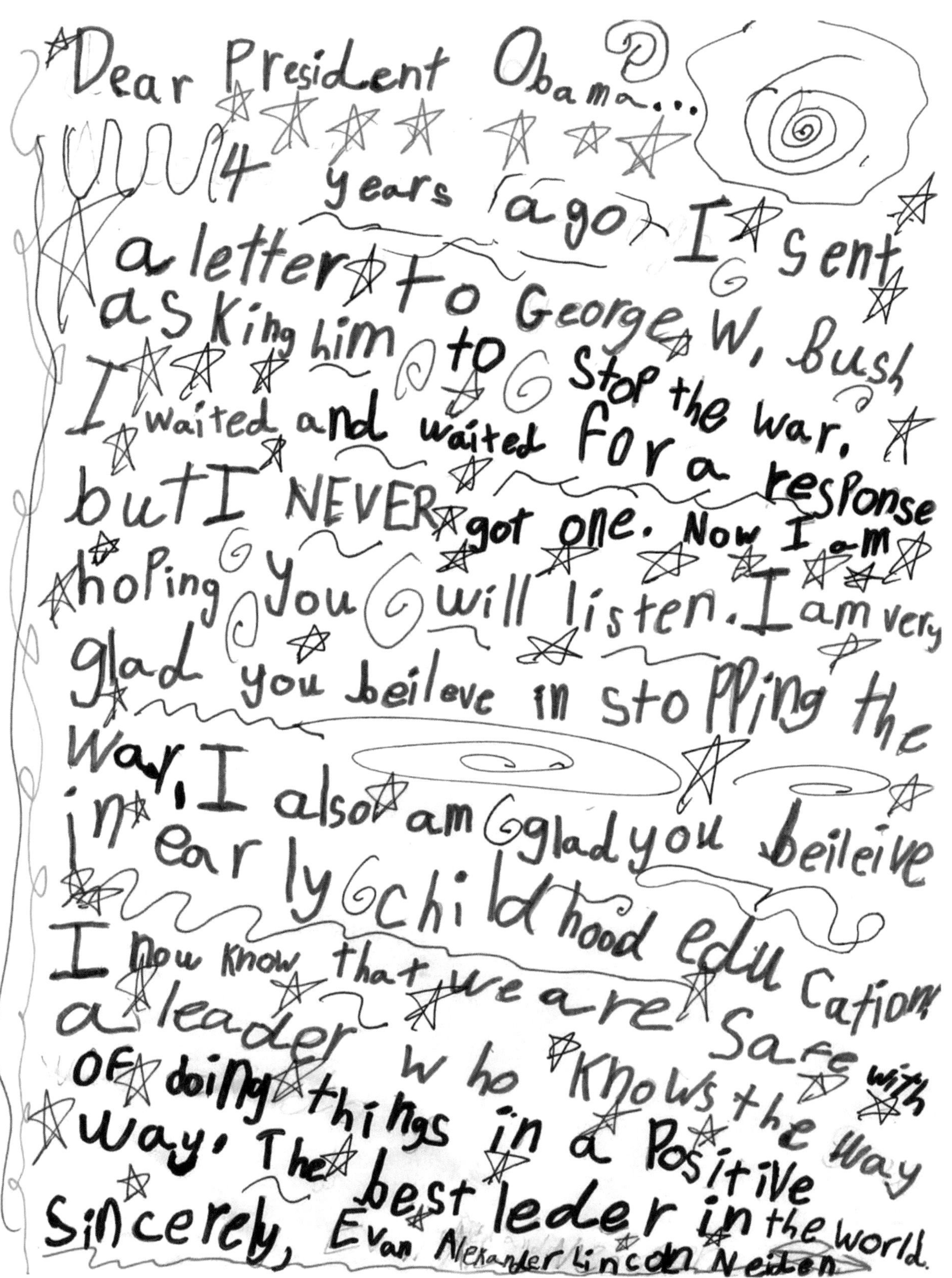

Dear President Obama...

4 years ago I sent a letter to George W. Bush asking him to stop the war. I waited and waited for a response but I NEVER got one. Now I am hoping you will listen. I am very glad you beileve in stopping the war. I also am glad you beileive in early childhood education. I now know that we are safe with a leader who knows the way of doing things in a positive way. The best leder in the world.

Sincerely, Evan Alexander Lincoln Neiden

EVAN ALEXANDER LINCOLN NEIDEN, 9, NEW YORK, NEW YORK

Dear President-Elect Obama,

I would really like you to stop the war in Iraq. I want you to stop the war because people are fighting and they can die. I know somebody who is fighting in Iraq. His name is Mick. He is one of my friends' dads. He is a soldier. I want him to stop fighting the war because he might get hurt. I want him to come home. Could you please stop the war?

Love,

Gabriel Hoffman (age 7)

GABRIEL HOFFMAN, 7, ROOSEVELT, NEW JERSEY

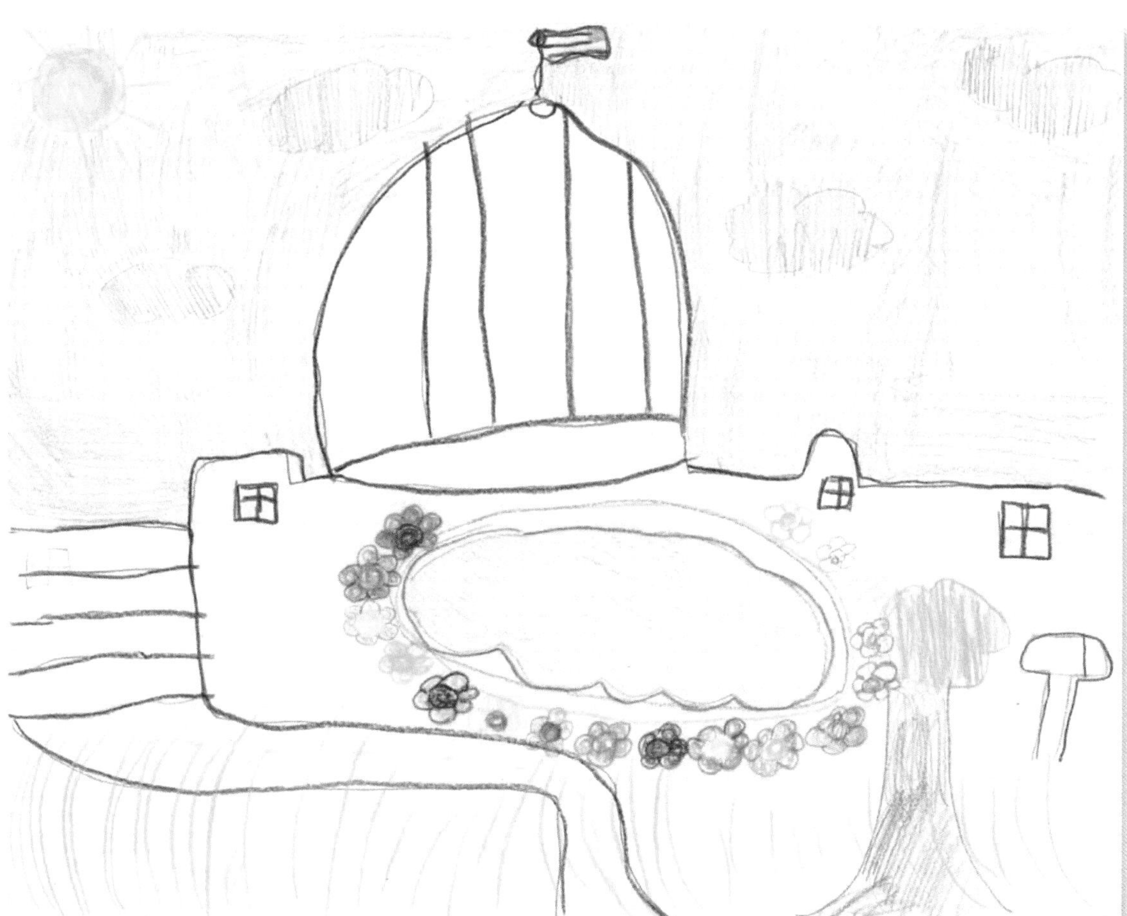

ALLYSON ROSE GORDON, 8, HIGHLAND PARK, ILLINOIS

Mackenzie Donahue

Dear President-elect Barack Obama,

My name is Mackenzie Donahue, and I am 11 years old. I don't know much about the presidential election and all that, but what I do know is that you can help our economy if you do these following things

1. Don't dump all the sewage into the ocean! How would you feel if someone just came in and dumped a whole truckload of garbage into your home?! Instead, turn all the sewage into compost and help the soil.

2. Money is made out of paper, and I bet the USA Mint makes over 100 billion dollars a day--that's wasting about 100 billion trees a day! To help save the trees, make money out of recycled paper!

3. Get scientists working on what the atmosphere is made out of--so when they find out, maybe we could add onto it! That way, one day the world might not fall apart and people won't have to live in space

4. Make people more aware of what's going on and how bad the economic crisis is, and tell them how they can help and make everything better! Like re-use paper instead of saying, "Oh, no! There's a mark on my paper! I better throw it out!" Use the back, get white-out and cover the mark --don't just throw it out. It's useable! Also, you can get the schools to start helping recycle, like in my school. We have recycling bins for empty bottles and cans, Make all schools realize what's going on, and maybe they might get recycling bins, too!

Also, think about it. I am 11 years old and I already know what we can do to help out our economy, and people even 80 years older than me don't know what's going on or how they can fix it!

There are also ways you can help families! Most people don't have a home or don't even have a family. But what you can do to help is, maybe the community could start programs that invite anybody to come to you home for no fee, and have fun and hang out and do activities!

Thank you for taking your time to listen to me complain about how bad our economy is, and how we can fix it. Hopefully I can meet you some day.

Sincerely,
Mackenzie Donahue

MACKENZIE DONAHUE, 11, NEWTON, MASSACHUSETTS

Dear President Obama,
You are the final piece of the puzzle. You can, and have, inspired people like no one I have ever seen before. With you, we can change the way the world looks at us. But, it's not just about image; it is about fixing the problems that we have created. It is about making a better world for generations to come. About getting care for those who need it. It's about finding a new energy source because, without one, we won't have a planet anymore. It is about stopping children from being orphaned by war. It is about letting it be known that all men and women are created equal, and that people should not be discriminated against based on race, gender, sexual preference, and religion. It is not about me or you; it is not about America alone, but the world as a whole. And with you, I think we can change it for the better. —Sincerely, Bridgette Kluger

BRIDGETTE KLUGER, 13, NEW YORK, NEW YORK

Dear President Obama,

Congratulations on winning the election. With you as the president this country can move in a different direction. Here is a checklist of issues to address as president:

- ☐ Stop deforestation and oil drilling in Alaska
- ☐ Stop the war in Iraq
- ☐ Help ease the financial crisis
- ☐ Help homeless people all across America
- ☐ Improve the pollution situation everywhere
- ☐ Stop terrorists all across the world
- ☐ Get fresh water and food to people in need
- ☐ Give everyone health care
- ☐ Have bettter education for everyone
- ☐ Get more people to use renewable energy sources such as solar, water, and wind-powered energy.

I am not expecting you to solve all of these problems, but America would be a much better place if you could even solve half of these.

When my family was downstairs talking about world-wide politics I was watching the election special on T.V. and I kept bringing them updates on the election.

Best of luck,

Mateo Lopez-castillo
12 years old
Brooklyn, NY

MATEO LOPEZ-CASTILLO, 12, BROOKLYN, NEW YORK

Dear Barack Obama,
You are the best President ever! You should be President for 8 years instead of 4. I wish you good luck. And one more thing, Can you write back?

Sincerely,
Josh Winston

JOSHUA WINSTON, 9, MONTCLAIR, NEW JERSEY

Dear Barak Obama,
I am so happy that you are going to be our new president! Can you please make a childrens day because there is a mothers day and a fathers day. And then we can have a realy fun day!

from,
Hannah

HANNAH LAMMIN, 8, MONTCLAIR, NEW JERSEY

HARRISON HEINRICH, 10, DWIGHT, ILLINOIS

Dear, Mr. pres. elect Obama.

Me and my sisters have always wanted you to win. When you did win I knew I have had the privlage to Be alive during presidential history. I Love it how you said that "we always think the only history in Presidents are past us" and you said "we can change". I belive you will have a huge Impact on the contry. I have wacthed your speech online at least three times, its so powerful and great.

Proud to write this to you

Harrison Bret Heinrich

I am 10 Years old

Dear President Obama,

You can help people with your stuff. You can do everything. If you need help with it, you can ask for help. My mommy, my daddy, or me.

Your friend,

RACHEL HOUSE, 5, MONTCLAIR, NEW JERSEY

Dear President Barack Obama,

Congratulations! You are the 44th president! Everyone in Hawaii is so happy that you were elected president. I saw your speech the morning when you became president. My family kept clapping and my Grandma said that the speech was perfect.
Good luck!
From, Zack

ZACHARY BRUNN, 8, HONOLULU, HAWAII

KYLA YAMASHITA, 8, HONOLULU, HAWAII

Dear President Barack Obama,

I am glad that you are the new president of the United States because you were born in Hawaii and I was too. I hope that you will have fun being the president. I think that you would make a good leader for our country. I like your oath that you said in the inauguration. Have lots of fun!
From,
Kyla Yamashita

Dear President Barack Obama,

Congratulations! You're the 44th president of the United States! I just know that you're going to be a great president! My friend Sydnie's Dad's sister went to your school and was your classmate in Punahou! You would prebrably remember your Classmate from Punahou, right?
Sincerely,
Jacey Moriguchi

JACEY MORIGUCHI, 8, HONOLULU, HAWAII

NYAGAAK DENG, 5, LINCOLN, NEBRASKA

"We have an obligation and a responsibility to be investing in our students and our schools. We must make sure that people who have the grades, the desire and the will, but not the money, can still get the best education possible."
—Barack Obama

november 23, 2008

Dear Mr. Obama,

Congratulations on winning the election I voted for you in my school election, I got to use a real voting machine! Anyway, 60% of the school votes were for you. I don't think any other election has influenced so many kids, including me. Color barriers have finally been broken. Who knows, maybe next term we'll have a hispanic, chinese, indian, or woman president! The best part is, you weren't elected because you're african American, you won because you're the best man for the job. You're smart, kind, responsible, trustworthy, and inspiring. You inspire people to do things themselves, instead of waiting for someone else to do it. Though you might be the right person for the job, no one said their term would be easy.

Mr. Bush has left us in a 3 billion dollar deficit, a problem that might lead to a second great depression. This is a very difficult problem to fix. But America believes you can fix it It may not be easy, but I say in the words of America's next great president,

Yes you can!

Anna Bloomfield
Westfield, New Jersey
12 years old

ANNA BLOOMFIELD, 12, WESTFIELD, NEW JERSEY

Dear Obama,
I hope you are the greatest President ever.
I hope you change the World!

Love,
Zoey
Age 7
Brithday April 8Th 2001

ZOEY DILLON LEVINE, 7, NEW YORK, NEW YORK

STUDENTS FROM URBANA MIDDLE SCHOOL
FREDERICK, MARYLAND

MEREDITH WHEELOCK, 13

One thing you need to improve is the poverty here in America. Lots of people in the united states are suffering and being stuck in poverty. Choice or not by choice, these people are hungry and sometimes hurt. I think you should do something about that.

ALEXA MIKK, 13

Mr. President:

May you please help our country out of this economic crisis?
Remember that even little things can help.

Please do not raise taxes.
Respect all people and listen to their opinions.
Everyone is in trouble and is worried about their jobs and money.
Someone needs to help and you are the man to start.
If you don't do something soon, the situation will get worse.
Don't procrastinate.
Enlist the help of your cabinet members.
Needless to say, the economy is in trouble and the American people need your help.
Take time and enjoy being president!

"There are now over a half a million people without jobs and homes. What is the answer to this **mind-boggling conundrum**? Invest in America. Take all the billions being used to finance the war and bail out companies that have filed for bankruptcy and use it to create more roads, educate kids and come up with more ways to turn America into a green nation. The more we invest in America, the more issues we can solve." —Ashwin Sekar, 12

"One issue is that concerns me is the No Child Left Behind Act. Standardized tests help some students, but hold back others who are gifted and talented. Teachers only teach to what is on these tests, which limits the amount of knowledge students can absorb... Thank you for taking the time to read this. I very much appreciate that you want to listen to our country's youth." –Katharine Tobler, 13

ANONYMOUS, 13

My biggest concern is that marijuana should be legalized. There is a lot of research and science that says that marijuana is less addictive than nicoteen. Marijuana is a plant and in my opinion, no plant should be illegal. When you make a plant illegal, it seems very communist does it not?

ANISH DALAL, 13

Another one of my concerns is the issue of how Americans are incapable of affording health care. Honestly, it stuns me how cruel the American health system can be by putting sick and wounded patients out on the street just because of a simple piece of paper. These are our citizens, the foundation of our nation that we simply toss aside. These issues need to be remedied, sir, and I believe you are the perfect one for the job.

"I believe kids should have a say in government. **Kids under 18** make up a great deal of the population. And while I know they can't be granted the right to vote, they should be able to speak and listen in Congress. We wouldn't have a final say or vote, but **our voices should be heard** just like American adults."

—Vergil Bandini, 12

EMMA BAKER, 13

I believe that America should be a place where we don't have to worry about every step we make. For example, five years ago people didn't have to worry about the price of food for the week as much as we do today. I think that we don't realize how much we have until it is all gone.

To persue change we need to think, create and most of all believe. It all started when Martin Luther King said, "I have a dream…" A small idea may eventually lead to a greater future.

CAMERON COLE, 13

Another big issue is the war in Iraq. I think we should fight until we find Al Qaeda. This is important to me because I lost a family member in 9-11.

"I am a seventh grader and an avid Obama supporter. When I grow up, I want to be a lawyer and the first Pakistani-American president of the Harvard Law Review and the United States of America. Just as you were the first African-American to hold these prestigious titles. If you ever want to know what Generation Y thinks, or just need a little help, I will do my proud duty as an American to help my country out. Call me." —Hamzah Raza, 12

ADDIE STRAUS, 13

For the economic crisis, I think you should re-build the roads, bridges, and more. This will make more jobs available to the public, and will re-create what Franklin Delano Roosevelt did during the Great Depression. I also think we need to normalize our relations with Cuba. The Cuban Missile Crisis occurred around 40 years ago. We could benefit greatly by trading with the Cubans; and people with perfectly reasonable reasons to go to Cuba can't, because of our relations with them.

J U L I A N   R O S E N B L U M

Dear Mr. President-Elect,

My name is Julian Rosenblum and I'm a seventh grader in a middle-class family. Being quite interested in politics, I have followed this election from the primary. From the beginning, I whole-heartedly supported you and I had and still have faith that you will turn our country around.

First off, I would like to congratulate you on your landslide victory and on making United States history by being the first African-American elected President.

I do, however, have something specific to ask of you. When you're in the oval office, you will be engulfed with responsibilities. Every word you speak will be heard by the country. This will be overwhelming for you but please, don't forget what you stand for.

Don't forget the values and issues that made you want to run for president.

Don't forget about the middle class like our last President did. I have faith that you will be one of the best Presidents this fine country has ever had.

Just remember, don't forget what you believe in. I wish you luck as we begin our journey. Please make my future brighter.

Yours truly,
Julian Rosenblum

JULIAN ROSENBLUM, 12, NEW YORK, NEW YORK

MAYA

Dear Barack,

I think you need to stop the Iraq war somehow (I was going to say we should have world peace, but this will help) and save the economy. We should also try to be as environmental as possible. If we reduce greenhouse gases, it would help the whole world.

One way to do this is by using fuel-efficient cars for public transportation and police. Electric cars should be reinvented. It would be nice if every student at every school had the opportunity to take the bus. Also, in some of the sunny states, solar panels could be used for power, and in windy places, wind turbines. Recycling is important, too, especially for glass, plastic and aluminum, because they aren't biodegradable. In Mexico, I saw garbage cans that said "organic" and "inorganic" (it was in Spanish, of course). That might also be good. In schools we should be educated about alternative energy so we can help.

When you are president, I don't want to go to other countries and meet people who hate America. It's important to me for you to improve the reputation of the U.S. because my parents make me travel to other countries a lot. When I was in Mexico almost everybody we talked to about you supported you because, as they said, "Whatever happens in America affects us too."

I'll see you at the inauguration. I'll be the girl from Alaska with a tie-dye that says "Yes we can" over my parka and a camera around my neck.

Sincerely,
Maya Heubner

CAMILLE

Dear Barack Obama,

I think all schools should have recycling stations. My school recycles batteries, and I think that's good. But that they should take it a step further, to recycling all recyclable materials. The only drawback is, What kid would want to haul their recycling to school? I certainly wouldn't, because I have too many other things to carry. Maybe parents could help by dropping off some recycling when they pick their kids up from school or when they're in the neighborhood. Also, the people who live nearby could use it as a recycling station for them, too.

Sincerely,

Camille Heubner, 11

CAMILLE HEUBNER, 11, ANCHORAGE, ALASKA

MAYA HEUBNER, 13, ANCHORAGE, ALASKA

Jan 2, 2009

Dear President Obama,

My name is Cole Pietsch.

I am seven years old.

I have a question for you.

I forget how many votes you got when you were running for President.

I like America being a free country and I want you to keep it that way.

Nothing worries me about you.

Please Pay close attention to people in America. They might have good ideas for you.

I can't think of anything else to say.

Bye for now.

Cole

COLE PIETSCH, 7, CARBONDALE, COLORADO

GABRIELLE HUSKO, 8, ROOSEVELT, NEW JERSEY

12/3/08

Dear President Elect Obama,

My name is Gabrielle Husko, and I want to tell you all about my fear of too many people polluting. Too many people are polluting and they're making global warming come quickly. I was thinking that maybe constuction workers could build garbage cans every block where there are lakes, rivers and dams. I hope you would agree with my idea. My idea will help the enviorment. Can you please use my idea?

From,
Gabrielle Husk

Dear President Obama,

My name is Zach Thomas and I go to Urbana Middle School in Frederick Maryland. I have a few things that I would like to see you do as president. I am not into politics very much but there are stiv some things that I see every day that needs change.

One thing that I would like you to change as president is to make playoffs in College football. I like Penn State and every year they come so close to the BCS Championship and then they lose 1 game like this year and the BCS drops their ranking so much that their hopes of a championship are crushed.

Also one thing that I would like you to do as President is get rid of puppy mills. I have a dog just like you and I have seen puppy mills before and how horrible they are.

And finally I would like you to do anything that will help North Carolina win the NCAA tournament. Just kidding!

Sincerely,
Zach Thomas

ZACH THOMAS, 12, IJAMSVILLE, MARYLAND

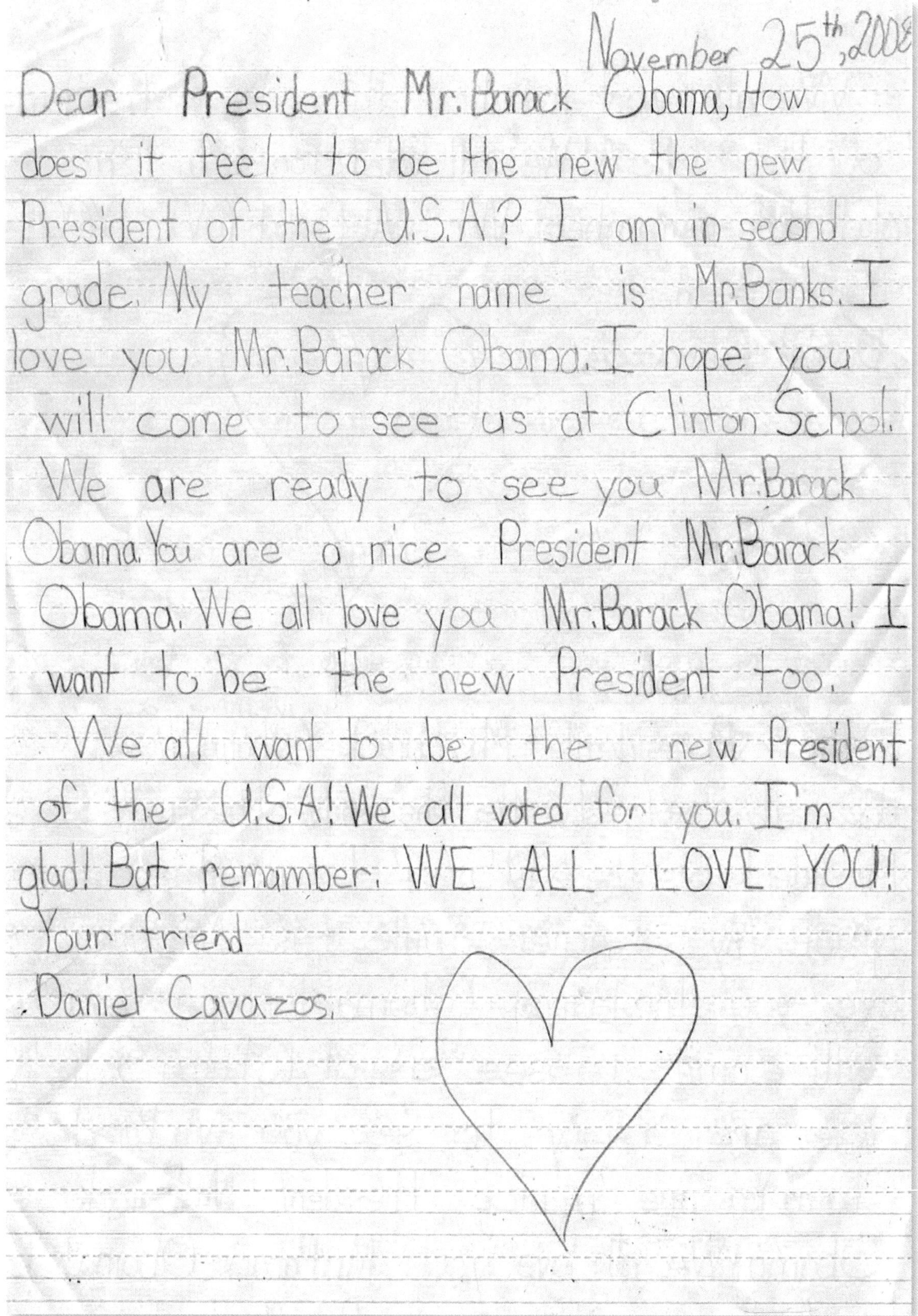

November 25th, 2008

Dear President Mr. Barack Obama, How does it feel to be the new the new President of the U.S.A? I am in second grade. My teacher name is Mr. Banks. I love you Mr. Barack Obama. I hope you will come to see us at Clinton School. We are ready to see you Mr. Barack Obama. You are a nice President Mr. Barack Obama. We all love you Mr. Barack Obama! I want to be the new President too.

We all want to be the new President of the U.S.A! We all voted for you. I'm glad! But remamber. WE ALL LOVE YOU!

Your friend
Daniel Cavazos.

DANIEL CAVAZOS, 7, LINCOLN, NEBRASKA

Dear President Barrack Obama,

I have an idea for you to put to mind. You should think about listening to kids around the ages of 12 to 15 and what they think they would do if they were in your shoes and how they can help because everyone has their own opinions and would like them to be heard. No one listens to kids! Kids care about what will happen when they come of age to start making their own path in the world. We have good ideas too. We see what is happening with the war in Iraq, how many companies have to get bailed out, all the families losing jobs and the poverty that is in the near future. We have learned what has happened in Africa and in some of the other third world country and we have seen how sad and depressed they are and how it make everyone feel inside. We must stop this from happening and it has to happen soon because these things are at your door step and they are going to start knocking.

We all have to work together to solve these problems. You need to count on us kids to help because we are the future. Can we fix it… yes we can!! TOGETHER!

Your friend from MD,
Patrick Smith

PATRICK W. SMITH, 12, IJAMSVILLE, MARYLAND

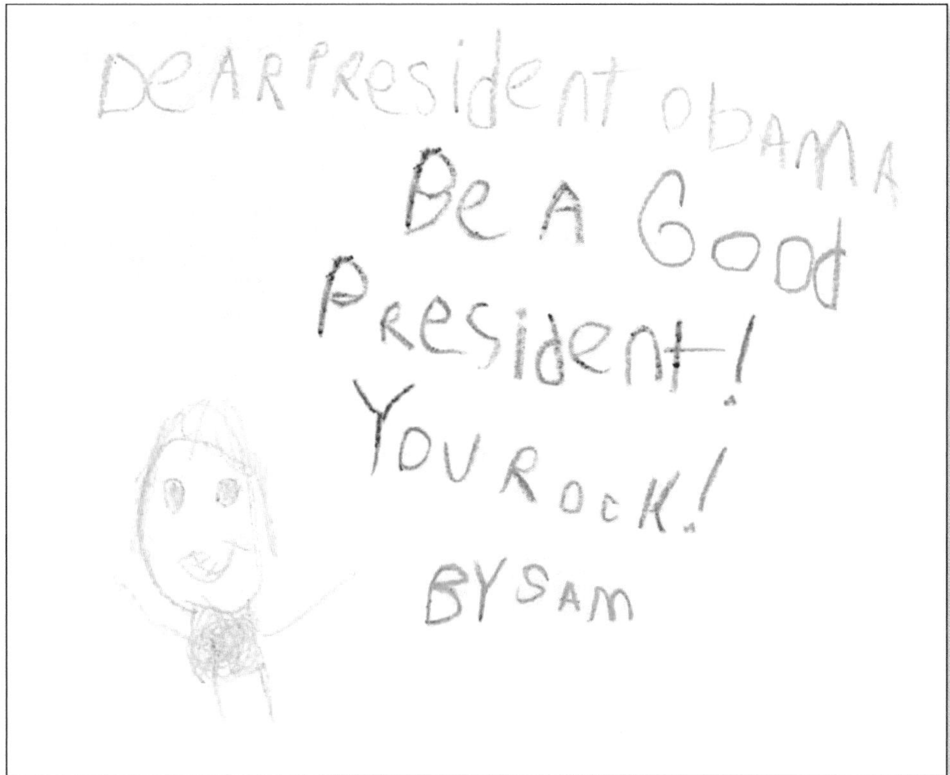

SAMUEL GOIDEL, 6, MONTCLAIR, NEW JERSEY

WILLIAM

Dear President Obama,

I have come up with some things that I think would be good for the country that I think you might want to try to use while you are president.

First, I think that we should use clean and reusable energy sources more, such as solar or wind. All of the energy emissions are destroying our ozone and creating global warming. If we don't stop burning so many fossil fuels our planet could end up like Venus! I don't think those would be very good living conditions.

Second, I used to live in Shaker Heights, Ohio, but over the summer we moved to Minnesota because there were no jobs in northeast Ohio. I felt sad that I left all of my friends behind, but I made lots of new friends here! I think that you could create new jobs to help people who are unemployed. That would help the economy because every time they got paid, they would spend their money on things like clothes or food, which will help the economy.

I hope you accomplish lots of good things for the country during your presidency. I would have voted for you if I could, but I am too young.

Sincerely,
William Beimers, Age 11
Northfield, MN

WILLIAM BEIMERS, 11, NORTHFIELD, MINNESOTA

Dear President Obama,

I dream that this country
won't be a place of war anymore.
I hope that one day the world will
be a place of peace and happiness.

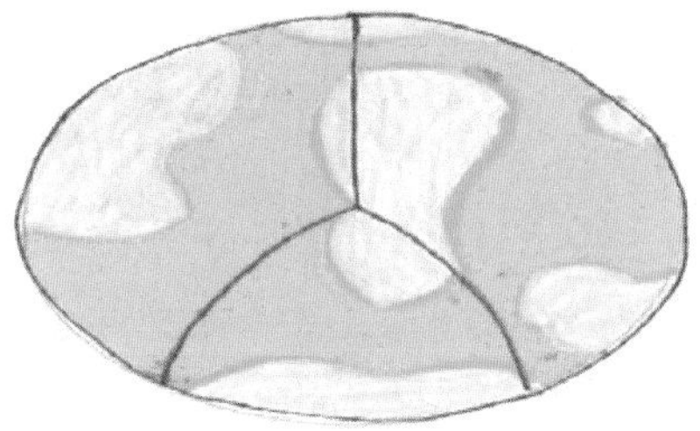

Andie Barber, Age 11,
Lansing, Michigan

ANDIE BARBER, 11, LANSING, MICHIGAN

ANTHONY NGUYEN, 7, LINCOLN, NEBRASKA

"If you're walking down the right path and you're willing to keep walking, eventually you'll make progress."
—Barack Obama

Dear President obama,

I always call you Rocky Balboa because it sounds just like your name. I always see you on t.v., and you are always talking to the people. I am proud because there has never been an African American president. I am proud because you are the same color as me. At our school vote, I voted for you! Good luck being our president and I hope I can meet you someday.

Sincerely,

Nyir Kuek

NYIR KUEK, 9, LINCOLN, NEBRASKA

Dear President Obama,

I hope you keep taxes low so my parents have more money to buy me toys. Congratulations on winning the election.

Love,
Jackson Woodard
Arden, N.C.

P.S. I hope you tell people to recycle. I'll tell people, too.

JACKSON WOODARD, 9, ARDEN, NORTH CAROLINA

Dear Mr. Obama,

Congratulations! I have some things to say about what you could do. The first thing is, that I think you should stop all the deforestation going around. Second of all, you should tell people about how much energy were wasting. Lastly, I just want you to remember that in some parts of the world they don't have clean water.

Mr. Obama, I want to tell how I think you're going to be an awesome president. The first thing is, when you talk in front of a crowd you look so calm. Second of all, your smile is very nice and inviting. Third of all, you talk to people less fortunate. I feel like if I knew you, I could trust you like I trust a friend.

Good luck,
Emily B
Westfield N.J.
Age 8

EMILY BLOOMFIELD, 8, WESTFIELD, NEW JERSEY

I'M PROUD TO BE AN AMERICAN

Dear President-Elect Obama,

First off I would like to congratulate you on your win. I think you ran a great campaign and disserve to be president. I'm very excited to see what action you take when you're finally in the White House.

I would like to thank you for taking time to read this letter. To be honest with you, I'm not exactly a politics fan. My family doesn't put signs up in our yard or fight with people when they disagree with us on politics. I'm a Democrat, but my best friend is a Republican. Now that I think about it, I'm not really a Democrat. In my opinion, politics is so complicated, I don't see how children like me can decide if they are a Democrat or a Republican.

After the election, I'd walk down the halls and hear people yell, "Yay, Obama won!" Then someone would reply, "Boo, Obama!" (I hope you take no offense at this.) This annoys me because I bet that they are just saying that because that's what their parents want them to say. I am a firm believer in believing in something for *your* reasons and not someone else's. That is why I'm going to say to you now that I'm not against you, but I'm not for you either. I believe that as long as you do good things for our country, I will be proud to call you my President.

I wish you luck and encourage you to make smart choices. For the record, I'm not just agreeing with you on some of the topics above so that you'll like me. I truly agree with your choices. At the moment I'd like to tell you that, in the words of one of my favorite songs, "I'm proud to be an American."

Signed, Sealed, and Delivered,
Cori Ritchey
7th grader at Cooper Middle School
McLean, Virginia

CORI RITCHEY, 12, GREAT FALLS, VIRGINIA

December 4, 2008

Dear President Elect Obama,

My name is Hunter Zimmerman and I am a third grader. I am against hunting. Do you hunt?

I am against hunting because I feel bad for animals. Baby animals die because hunters kill them and they cannot run fast enough.

Could you create a law that you must eat the meat if you hunt and kill it?

I am happy that I sent you this letter.

From,
Hunter

HUNTER ZIMMERMAN, 8, ROOSEVELT, NEW JERSEY

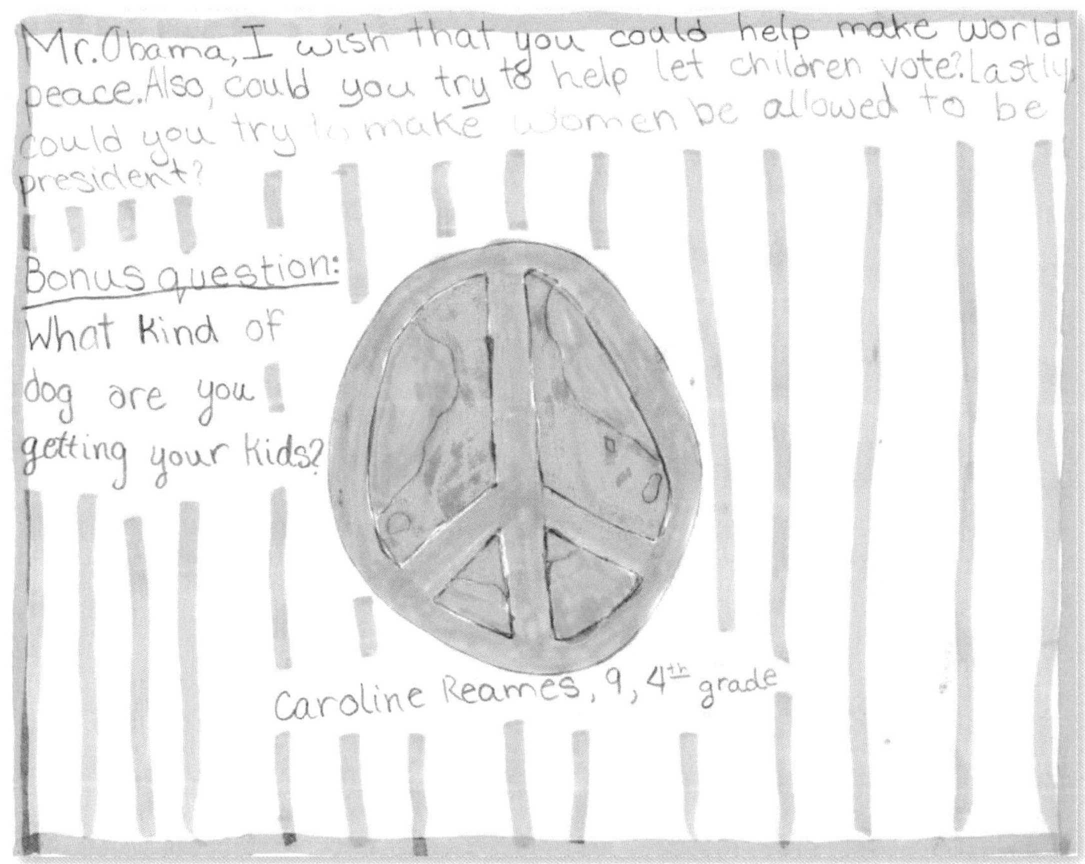
Mr. Obama, I wish that you could help make world peace. Also, could you try to help let children vote? Lastly could you try to make women be allowed to be president?

Bonus question:
What kind of dog are you getting your kids?

Caroline Reames, 9, 4th grade

CAROLINE REAMES, 9, FLAGLER BEACH, FLORIDA

JAMES

December 3, 2008

Dear President-elect Barack Obama:

Congratulations to you. Before you announced you were running for president, let's just say I knew more about new movies and TV shows than I did about politics. But having been raised in Illinois, I knew who you were. My parents followed your campaign when you ran for Senate. They also called me in to watch your speech at the Democratic National Convention.

So when you announced your presidential candidacy, I started to pay close attention to the race. I followed you every step of the way and got really involved in the process. I never realized debating with friends over politics was so much fun. I enjoy and take inspiration from your speeches (I've just joined the debate team at my high school, so I could use some pointers). In these past years, there has been too much fighting going between the Democrats and Republicans. I hope you will ease this bickering and unite the people of this great country.

Thank you for taking the time to read my letter, and good luck in the years to come!

Yours truly,

James Liebenson

JAMES LIEBENSON, 15, HIGHLAND PARK, ILLINOIS

December 4, 2008

Dear President-Elect Obama,

My name is Aimee. I would like to use this letter for two things. First, I'd like to congratulate you on becoming the next president. Next I would like to inform you on one issue that I find very important.

One issue I find very important to me, is gay marriage. Some states dont allow two people of the same gender to get married. Why? Isn't this America, a "free" country? If 2 people truly love each other then why not allow them to get married? Based on the first ammendment it says American citizens are free people. If weare "free", why can't two people of the same gender get married when abortion is allowed? I just don't understand your ~~your~~ perception of the constitution is. Why is this happening in the "free" country?

I hope this issue is one you adress as our new president. Thank you for reading my letter Mr. President.

Sincerly,
Aimee ♡

AIMEE FAULKNER, 13, FREDERICK, MARYLAND

Dear president obama,

I am 8 years old and I live in Green Bay WI. Now that you are president. I hope you will think about homeless people. I have a nice home with 4 bedrooms and 4 bathrooms. I know that some people don't have a nice home like mine. when I'm in chicago, I see people on the streets. They usualay have all their stuff with them. They look dirty, Hungery and tired and it makes me sad. My Daddy says a lot of homeless people used to be soilders. Some of them fought in wars. They served their country well. Now I think its time we take care of them. President odama, I hope that you will be able to find a way to help homeless people find a safe place to live.

Anna

ANNA LAYNE GOOLSBY, 8, DE PERE, WISCONSIN

Dear President Obama,

Thank you for being our President.

I am 9 years old. It has always been my dream to be a veternarian. I want you to change the world by saving the poor cute animals. After that you don't need to do anything.

Sincerely,
Judy Truong

JUDY TRUONG, 9, LINCOLN, NEBRASKA

Dear Mr. Obama,

I know you will be a great president! I think there should be more bookstores and librarys.

Sincerely,
Corinna D.

CORINNA DAVIS, 8, MONTCLAIR, NEW JERSEY

ROOSEVELT PUBLIC SCHOOL

ROOSEVELT, NEW JERSEY

December 4, 2008

Dear President Elect Obama,

My name is Trevor Kosa and I'm a 9 year old 3rd grade student in Roosevelt Public School. I think there should be a Kids Day when kid get to have fun all day. There's a Mother's Day, a Father's Day and what about kids? If there was a Kid's Day, and it was on a school day, we would have no homework. The day would consist of having a party. The party would consist of playing math, social studies, language arts and reading games.

Please make this happen President Elect Obama!

From,
Trevor

TREVOR KOSA, 9

12/4/08

Dear President Elect Obama,

My name is Crystal Raines. I am in third grade. I'm eight years old and I go to Roosevelt Public School. I would like you to think of ways to stop people who are hurting other children or people. I didn't like it when I heard that this nice man was opening a door at Walmart and was killed. A crowd of people piled on top of the man, with the door on top of him. I would not like this to happen again. What can we do?

Signed,
Crystal Raines

CRYSTAL RAINES, 8

12/3/08

Dear President Elect Obama,

My name is Emily Ng. I want to help you think about ideas so children can help protect the environment. Maybe you could declare a day called Children Can Help Day. On this day kids can go around watering plants, picking up garbage that people threw on the ground, and to collect old clothing from people to give it to the poor. You can use kids, use them because all kids have time to work on things. You can ask kids to make more garbage cans around the world. Then people will see the cans and not throw their garbage on the ground. Do you think my idea is good?

Sincerely,
Emily Ng

EMILY NG, 8

Dear President Elect Obama

My name is Aaron Muzer and I am a third grader. Do you know how people get hurt in cities because of crimes? Well I sort of have an idea to help. Could you place cameras in cities to protect people? I know how you can get cameras. You can get money from taxpayers. I know they will agree.

From,
Aaron Muzer

AARON MUZER, 9

12/4/08

Dear President Elect Obama,

My name is Angelica Majorczyk and I am eight years old. I am a third grade student at Roosevelt Public School. I have a fear about what occurred on Black Friday. Some people got up at 5 am to go shopping. A doorman who worked at a Walmart was opening a door. A group of people then pushed down the door and it fell on the doorman. No one stopped to help him. All the people just plowed all over him. He died. When I heard this I felt sad and mad. How could someone be so selfish just so they could get something first? I think we could prevent this from happening by having a few security guards to keep the mob of people in order before there is a big sale.

I know that I am only 8 years old, but I think my idea could help prevent this accident from happening again.

From,
Angelica Majorczyk

ANGELICA MAJORCZYK, 8

12-04-08

Dear President Elect Obama,

My name is Carson Donnelly-Fine and I care a lot about animals. I wrote a letter to President George Bush about how they take baby animals away from their moms and dads just for people's entertainment. I think that they should limit the amount of baby animals that are used to one or two. Afterwards, the animals should be brought back to the wild. Animals have feeling but they just can't tell us.

From,
Carson

CARSON DONNELLY-FINE, 8

Dear President Obama,

Can you shut down cigarett stores because people smoke every year to be cool and then they die. If people show other people then they get addicted and keep smoking smoking in front of the family. Then it is hard for them to breath. If you do it in front of baby's they proboly would start coughing. A person keep's on smoking your lungs will turn black. Thanks for listening

Your friend,
Tommy
Nguyen

TOMMY NGUYEN, 9, LINCOLN, NEBRASKA

TARA

Dear Mr. Obama,

After a couple months of class projects, yelling down the hallway "GO OBAMA!" and presenting in debates why I thought you were best, you won! I have to say I was really excited when I found out about that. I was watching CNN in my room, making a shirt to wear the next day that said, "OBAMA 2009-2013" -- and then all of a sudden I saw that guy on the TV, sitting behind the desk with little cards in his hand. He took a short breath and said that you had won California -- and that you were the new president of the United States!

I ran to my parents and yelled "MOM, DAD AHHH! OBAMA WON! HE WON!!" I couldn't believe it. I was ecstatic, not only because you won, but because I watched history happen, right in front of my eyes! Something I could tell my family in the future. My kids and my grandkids.

I watched all of the debates between you and Mr. McCain. I saw all of your commercials, and smiled every time I saw an Obama sticker or poster. I listened to all pf your plans for our future. They're great!

One of your plans that I especially like is the plan to bring the troops back from Iraq. I feel that not only are a lot of Americans' tax dollars being spent on the war, but people are losing their loved ones in a war that seems like it will never end. Bringing the troops back is a good idea, and sooner or later, most people who doubt that will think again.

Another one of your plans that made my family and me happy is your plan for Iran. Both of my parents were born in Iran, and I visit there every other summer. I love being there with my family and friends. One thing that would hurt me so much is not being able to see my family again because of war. Mr. Obama, maybe the government isn't that great, but the people shouldn't get punished. I've seen what's happened to families in Iraq, and I would be hopeless if that happened to mine.

I think you'll be a great president sir. I hope you inspire people to always keep their minds open, and not to judge someone so easily. I know that you and Mr. McCain want the best for this country, and that's really all that matters. You opened up my eyes to see that black, white, Muslim, Catholic, Jewish, or anything -- it doesn't matter. If you follow your dreams and stick to them, you can achieve anything.

You achieved your goal and that is awesome. Good job sir, and congratulations!

Tara Hosseini
8th Grade

TARA HOSSEINI, 13, GREAT FALLS, VIRGINIA

ZOË REAMES, 15, FLAGLER BEACH, FLORIDA

“Yes we can.”
—Barack Obama

EMILY DANIELLE

Dear President Obama,

I am an 11-year-old girl living in La Crescenta, California. I was thrilled when you got elected for president because I trust you to make our nation better. I believe that, in your hands, our nation will grow better and better every day.

As a kid I want to have a promising future, and I believe that you can give that to me. One thing that I hope you can do is help the economy. I try to go as green as possible, and I hope that you will get this nation to do the same. I also think that you and I want the same thing for the economy.

One other thing that I think would be wise for you to do is to bring the troops home. They have been working to hard for TOO long. The troops are regular people who deserve more than they are getting right now. Lots of people have been killed in battle, not to mention lots of people who were just walking by at the wrong time. I believe that you can help bring these Americans home to their families and friends.

I KNOW that you will take all these things into consideration, and I will be happy when you do. All I want is a peaceful future for me and for future generations!

Sincerely,
Emily

EMILY KLUGER, 11, LA CRESCENTA, CALIFORNIA

Dear Obama!!!

Do your children like to do crafts?

I liked the puppy speech. There is a book called "What presidents are made of." It is a very funny book!

A president needs a brain to think well.

Happy President time!!!

Dora Luna neiden

DORA LUNA NEIDEN, 7, NEW YORK, NEW YORK

Dear Mr. Obama,
My name is Claire. I have alot of favorite things. Some of them are doing ballet, hunting ghosts and playing musical instruments.
Here are my questions for you:
How are you going to make this Continent greener?
Can you fix this economy?
How are you going to help me and my mom, who is now single keep enough money in our pocket to buy food?
Will you keep the arts alive?
and most importantly...
Do you believe in ghosts?

Claire Mortenson
Ogden, Utah
age 11

CLAIRE MORTENSON, 11, OGDEN, UTAH

January 11, 2009

Dear President Obama,

I was brought up to be not only a proud American citizen but a citizen of the world, and with you as our president I truly believe that every child can be proud to say they are American. The pride I felt on election night resonated throughout the world and will continue to be felt throughout your presidency. I believe that you represent the best parts of America. On a personal level, my dream for America is to be once again regarded as a free and accepting nation, not one looked down upon by other countries -- a country where anyone and everyone can achieve their goals and dreams if they are willing to work hard enough for them. I look forward to once again being a country that, under your leadership, can work like a team, to improve the well being of our citizens and people everywhere.

Americans are often stereotyped as close-minded and nationalistic and I am proud that as our president you do not fall into this or any other negative stereotypes. It is good to be able to feel like your president can relate to you, and that he has respect for each and every American. I believe you have the qualities that everyone should strive to have: hard-working, dedicated, respectful, intelligent, full of integrity, worldly, and open-minded.

I have been raised in a household that understands the importance of having a balance between national pride and inter-nationalism. While I am an American, born and raised in Georgia, I attend an International School and have been fortunate enough to travel abroad and expand my horizons. I think that is why I feel it is so important for Americans to have a broader understanding of the world and the desire to be a part of not only a national community, but a global one.

It is my hope that you and your administration can encourage the joy of learning across the country, because it is education after all that creates opportunity and lays the foundation for a future of peace, tolerance and cooperation between people and nations of the world.

I feel that thanks to you we are entering a new time filled with diverse and wise leaders and hope for the future. I greatly anticipate voting for your re-election which will also be my first time voting.

Congratulations and thank you for all the work you have done already. Best wishes in your presidency.

Sincerely,

Nicole Dancz
10th Grade
Atlanta International School
Atlanta, GA

NICOLE KATHLEEN DANCZ, 15, ATLANTA, GEORGIA

LIAM...

Dear President Obama,

I think people produce way too much trash. Some ways to lessen that amount are to use fabric shopping bags and to recycle what you can. I wish more people would do this.

Liam

Age 10, Vermont

LIAM BELIVEAU, 10, ST. GEORGE, VERMONT

...AND DILLON

Dear President Obama,

I've heard a lot of people say that they want to reduce our dependency on foreign oil, but I feel that we need to reduce our dependency on oil, period. I know that there isn't a miracle alternative energy—every area needs its own source. I hope you can get this country off oil in the next eight years.

—Dillon, Age 14, Vermont

DILLON BELIVEAU, 14, ST. GEORGE, VERMONT

11-29-08

Dear Obama,

You rock! I wish I could have seen you on TV because I really wanted to watch you on TV because my bed time is 8:45 and I wanted to watch the election. I want you to do these things I'm going to tell you.

1. make better water for people who have dirty water

2. make white people who hate black people care about homeless black people and regular black people like you.

3. help the environment by no smoking in the subway.

Sencirly,
Julian
Age: 8 (almost 9)

JULIAN LOPEZ-CASTILLO, 8, BROOKLYN, NEW YORK

STUDENTS FROM MS. FARRELL'S CLASS

COOPER MIDDLE SCHOOL

McLEAN, VIRGINIA

"Congratulations! You have finally broken the final racial boundary for African Americans! It must be overwhelming to be you; even the smartest person in the entire world would be trembling in their boots. But, you are a very good man and I know you will restore America's pride."

— Adam Pardo, 13

"Congratulations! You're now the leader of the free world and the symbol of America, the greatest country in the world. Yes, despite all of these problems we've been having, I still believe that, and I will continue to believe that forever. America is freedom, America is hope, America is the land of the brave! While I am not entirely sure where my path leads, I know exactly what I picture America to be for the rest of my life and for my children's children. Are you up to the job, Mr. Obama?"

— Hannah M. Engler, 14

"Have you ever thought of using video games to help the economy? I, as a gamer, would be good with that. Video games aren't all that bad. There is a difference between being insane about video games and just liking them. Just speaking honestly."

— Alix Nyden, 12

"There is an old Indian proverb that says, 'We do not inherit the world from our parents, we borrow it from our children.' That's what I think about when I think about America. I congratulate you on your success. Cooper Middle School is counting on you, and we're cheering for you all the way!"

— Ashley Leah Johnson, 13

I just want to say CONGRATULATIONS!! I mean, I've won a guitar in a raffle, but winning the role of president is truly amazing!"

— Jenna Dean, 14

"The thing I fear the most about the government is Democratic majority. I think if you don't support any ideas Republicans thought up, you and Congress will wipe out the Republicans. You may have won the election, but 47% of the country still votes Republican. So please don't exclude 47% of the nation."

— Brendan Cafferky, 13

"I think it's totally cool that I have the same name as your daughter!"

— Malia Berner, 13

TRACE HEFNER, 7, HIGHLAND PARK, ILLINOIS

"You will always be remembered as the first African American president, but make the world remember you for something else: being the best president of the United States of America."

— Robby Byrne, 14

COOPER MIDDLE SCHOOL

"Congratulations on being elected America's 44th president! I never thought I'd be able to say those words to you, but you really shocked me with your heroics—you showed the world what an underdog can do. America is not just a world power—it is my home, the place where I know I belong. I've been so fortunate to be brought up in a land of freedom, equality and happiness. I know you will fulfill your duties by making America a perfect nation."
— Taymour Hashemzadeh, 13

"When I look up into space at night, I feel a sense of content, because I know this liberty might not be enjoyed in other countries. It is an honor to live in the greatest nation in the world. Your winning the election turned a new page in history and filled our hearts with great hope."
— Chris Negiz, 14

"Congratulations on winning the presidency. It's great that we have finally broken through the race barrier. But please be bi-partisan. This won't work without complete cooperation from both parties."
— Matthew Anderson, 13

SHELBY AUERBACH, 8, HIGHLAND PARK, ILLINOIS

"Before this election, I didn't really know a lot about politics; but from watching the debates, I learned so much. I would like to congratulate you for winning this election and, at the same time, making American history."
— Naya A. Patel, 13

ERIC STEVEN RHUM, 8, HIGHLAND PARK, ILLINOIS

"Mr. Obama, I really care deeply about where America will end up at. I hope that you can help this country regain its glory—to a place where everybody is happy again; where adults don't have to constantly worry about losing their homes or losing all of their savings. I really do hope that America can once again be great."
— Shannon Keene, 13

"The first issue you might want to address is the environment. Well, to be more exact, the ozone layer. If we don't work harder to solve that issue, then we won't have a place to live. And would you like to be President of a country that doesn't exist anymore?"
— Brooke McDonough, 13

"What are your plans for America? What, to you, is the country's biggest problem? I think it is the war. I mean, it's simple logic: If we are dead, then we can't worry about the economy or immigration or whatever else there is to worry about. If I were you, I would put the war first."
— Reid Charbonnet, 12

COOPER MIDDLE SCHOOL

"Our nation's flag is the symbol of hope around the world, and I am proud to be an American. One day I hope to become a Marine. You follow in the footsteps of one of the best presidents this country's history: John F. Kennedy. You are a great teacher and speaker, and we need a strong leader and a government that the people can trust. You have a long and hard job ahead of you, but I know that you can do it."
— James C. Kennedy, 13

"When JFK said we would send a man to the moon, we did. The average age of the people in that room in Houston was 26—way younger than anyone would probably guess. That means they were 18 when JFK first said we would go. In the end, he had inspired those young people to go out, go to college, and study hard. You have the power to do the same. Please give my generation something to achieve!"
— Devon Maloney, 14

EDEN MANDELL, 7, HIGHLAND PARK, ILLINOIS

"Once I was proud to be an American, but now disaster has struck. We are in pointless war and a disastrous economic crisis. We struggle for money to get the things we need, not to mention the things we want. We need someone to help us with all of this. Will you be that person?"
— Keane Alavi, 12

"America is a place where everyone has the chance to become anything they want to be. I am a natural born American citizen, but my parents were born in Iran. When they were young, they both moved away from their families to the U.S. to get a better education. America stands for freedom. We show the world how anything is possible."
— Nicole Azmoudeh, 13

"Although all my family members are Korean, and we moved into the States not even half a year ago, this country is still special because I was born in here. One of the biggest changes facing America is racism. I mean no offense to anyone, but I was quite afraid when I first stepped into this country. I heard stories about discrimination and troubles in schools because of what race you are. But from the 2008 election, you have shown me that I had nothing to worry about, and I really thank you for that."
— Jenny Ryoo, 14

"I would like to express my feelings on your views about education. I think that you and Joe Biden make a good point when it comes to reforming No Child Left Behind. It would be great if you could find a way to improve the tests used to track our progress. I would also like to know more about your Zero to Five plan. I've looked into it on your website, and it sounds like it could have a positive impact on our nation's youth. So I am very interested in hearing more about it."
— Cole Forrer, 13

COOPER MIDDLE SCHOOL

"On January 20, 2009 you will be the head of our nation, running our country, our Chief Executive—"the big guy"—and you will represent the beautiful U.S to many other nations. This election really made me look at America with a different perspective. Think how much our nation has changed! One hundred and fifty years ago, we had slaves; about 40 years ago, African-Americans couldn't sit in the front of a bus. Look at how far we've come: an African-American being the LEADER of the U.S.A.! This all makes me very proud. America is truly a place where anything is possible. "
— Jenna Dean, 14

"America means a lot to me. We are a role model for the world, a symbol of hope when other countries need help, and a symbol of love when other countries need comfort. That makes me feel special."

"To me, the American dream is starting to blur. About 60 percent of my parents' day is spent working. But when payday comes, how much money are they really getting? Doesn't it seem logical that if a person spends the majority of his/her time working, that he/she should be rewarded fully, and not have half or more of their income taken from them?"
— Connor Welsh, 14

HANIA SIENKIEWICZ, 7, HIGHLAND PARK, ILLINOIS

"Our country symbolizes freedom of religion, assembly, press, petition and speech to the entire world, five freedoms that are an honor and a privilege to have. America also means honesty, respect and bravery, and I would like to keep it that way. My ideal America is a place where everyone has a good, well-paying job; where young adults who have the interest and potential to go to a good college—but can't pay for it—can still go to college; where no child goes to bed hungry, and has a safe, warm place to live. I understand it will be extremely difficult to do this, but that is my dream. Congratulations again, Mr. Obama, and I will see you at your inauguration."
— Lauryn K. Johnson, 13

"This is the first election that I've ever really paid attention to. It was also the first time that my dad went door to door, asking people to vote. That means my dad really, really wanted you to win! I did too. I know you are going to be a great leader. America means a lot to me. We are a role model for the world, a symbol of hope when other countries need help, and a symbol of love when other countries need comfort. That makes me feel special."
— Rachel Myers, 12

NOLAN ELIZA TOBIN, 6, MONTCLAIR, NEW JERSEY

"Let us be our brother's keeper, Scripture tells us. Let us be our sister's keeper. Let us find that common stake we all have in one another."

—Barack Obama

Dear Barak Obama,

I am Jamie Haughton. I am ten years Old. Soon I will be eleven. I live in Mill Valley, California.

I am not happy with the health Care system. I have Growth Hormone Deficiancy. My sister Kate is 21 and has been sick for three years. She had Guillan-Barre syndrome and then developed depression. My sister Steph is 18 and has another mental illness called Bipolar Disorder. They are both in Treatment Centers.

The insuranse Company did <u>NOT</u> pay for Kate to go to Pain Rehab. And it does <u>NOT</u> pay for either Stephs or Kates treatment Centers because those things have to do with Mental illnesses therefore they wont pay. At least they pay <u>some</u> for my shots I take for Growth Hormone Deficiancy.

Please CHANGE health Care.

Sincerely, Jamie Haughton ♥

JAMIE HAUGHTON, 10, MILL VALLEY, CALIFORNIA

Dear President Obama,

Greetings from the Frozen Tundra of Green Bay, Wisconsin!

As a ninth grader, one issue that is important to me is finding an answer to the problem of starvation and malnutrition among African children. Every day, my family and I are fortunate enough to have three meals. We are able to enjoy vegetables and fruits, grains and meats, and a proper diet helps us maintain our good health. I know I'm lucky to always have food on my table. Unfortunately, I know that many African children are not so fortunate.

In school, I've learned that most of the children who live in poverty in Africa barely get one meal each day. Most times that one meal consists of only rice and water. Rice is a grain that is necessary for proper nutrition, but it doesn't provide the necessary components of the food pyramid that are essential for good nutrition and health. Because of this lack of balance in their diet, I have heard that over 50% of these children suffer calcium, iron and zinc deficiencies. Surely there must be some way we can help these starving children.

Sometimes when I'm watching TV and see a picture of children starving in Africa, I feel depressed and feel like crying. I wonder if there is a way I can help. Now, since you are the new president of the greatest, most powerful country in the world, I feel sure that you can help find a solution for this terrible problem. I believe that change can occur when people who truly care work together for a solution, and President Obama, I'm sure that you care for these children, too.

Thank you for listening to me; I'm sure you'll be a great President.

Jessica Goolsby

JESSICA M. GOOLSBY, 15, DE PERE, WISCONSIN

November 26, 2008

Dear Barack Obama,

It will be great to have you for a president. I think you should be a good president so people will think that it is good to have an African-American president. A lot of people voted for John McCain, but you were much better, and your votes were higher.

I will want to see you play basketball. I would like for you to help the homeless people and find out how to teach them and the kids who do not go to school.

I will like to be president maybe some day. It sounds interesting.

I hope you have fun!!!!!

From Ashley Fulton
Age 7
PepperPike, Ohio

Be a great president!

You McCain Palin

ASHLEY FULTON, 7, PEPPER PIKE, OHIO

sarah

Dear President Obama,

I believe you will be a wonderful president of our country. I think you have the potential to change America for the better. Some people just forget to realize how difficult your job can be, and think it is just a walk in the park for a president. Though I have never gone through the leadership you have partaken, I can pretty well guess that your job will not be the easiest in the world.

I would like to bring up a few matters concerning my thoughts as an American and a future voter. First of all, I would like to say that I am a Christian. I go to a Christian Academy, but I have also gone to a public elementary school. There were children there who believed the same as I did, and everyone seemed all right with that. But now it seems like the public schools are headed in a direction where students will not be allowed have a Bible in their book bag or to pray over their lunch meat. In the future, when I have children who might go to a public school, I hope that they will not get in trouble for a simple act of studying Scripture or praying for a friend.

Secondly, as a survivor of Stage IV neuroblastoma, a cancer of the nervous system, I would like to say that I am very grateful for the medicines and treatments I have received. But I feel that future victims of the horrible thing called cancer could be cured in a shorter amount of time and in an easier way if more funds were donated to pediatric cancer research. Even wonderful organizations give less than 5% of their proceeds to the pediatric side of cancer research. Also, many cancer treatments are first developed for adults then given as a sort of hand-me-down to children. Multiple young patients have worsened and even died from this practice.

–Sarah Smith

SARAH SMITH, 13, SMITHFIELD, NORTH CAROLINA

JOSH STERNBERG

Dear President Obama,

This election I was one year shy of being able to vote, but I still chose to involve myself with the political process as much as possible. Since reading an article on you in *Rolling Stone* back in the start of your campaign, I was hopeful that, with your victory in the election, there could be a change in how Americans think about themselves in relation to the rest of the world.

In studying European and American history, one can find that America primarily exercised a policy of isolation for a while, focusing on prosperity and stability within the country. Since imperialism and both World Wars, that policy has changed. America has started to think of itself as an invincible immortal world power; nothing else could touch us.

Although I was young at the time, the events of September 11 brought to the forefront of American consciousness the reality of just how vulnerable we really are. The failures of communication between government agencies; the lack of communication between international intelligence agencies; an embarrassing system for background checks; and the overall failure of the American people to recognize how a questionable policy of military, political, and economic involvement in the Middle East could all lead to an attack on both American and "western" values, and on the people of the United States. Americans had stopped thinking they were the only players in this global game, and the destruction of American society was a threat no one could ignore. The actions of the administration were an insult to the American people. There was no real communication between the government and American citizens, and the invasion of a country that had nothing to do with the 9/11 attacks brought forth a question that, to me, meant it was time to change, or say goodbye: Is this the end of America as we know it?

Towards the end of your campaign, I examined the potential outcomes with great concern not only for my future, but for the future America which none of us now will live to see. The economic crisis and confirmation of a recession put the final nail in the Republican coffin, but I could still only hope for the best. After you won (on my birthday), I spoke with my father about why I trust you to lead this country away from the brink of destruction into a new future. I said you were intelligent, a quality I think can be overlooked in presidential candidates; and that you looked at the big picture, which is vital to our success in dealing with countries who think differently from Americans. But most of all, I said I trust you because, despite your lack of practical experience, you will surround yourself with people who have exactly that, and most important, you will listen to their advice.

I wish you nothing more than the best of luck. Your presidency will be a difficult one; the challenges you face are looming and numerous. But from one citizen to another, I can tell you that with your victory in the election, America has taken a step in the right direction, and we are behind you all the way.

Sincerely,
Josh Sternberg
Junior, High School

JOSH STERNBERG, 17, SUDBURY, MASSACHUSETTS

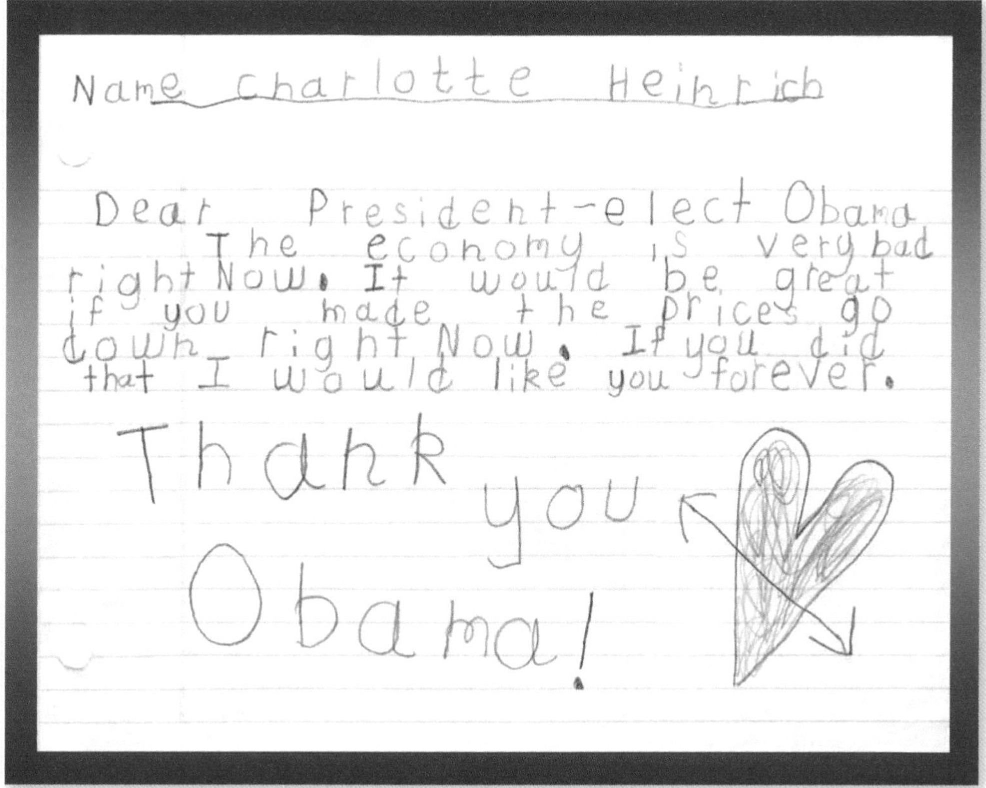

Name charlotte Heinrich

Dear President-elect Obama
The economy is very bad right Now. It would be great if you made the prices go down right Now. If you did that I would like you forever.

Thank you Obama!

CHARLOTTE HEINRICH, 7, DWIGHT, ILLINOIS

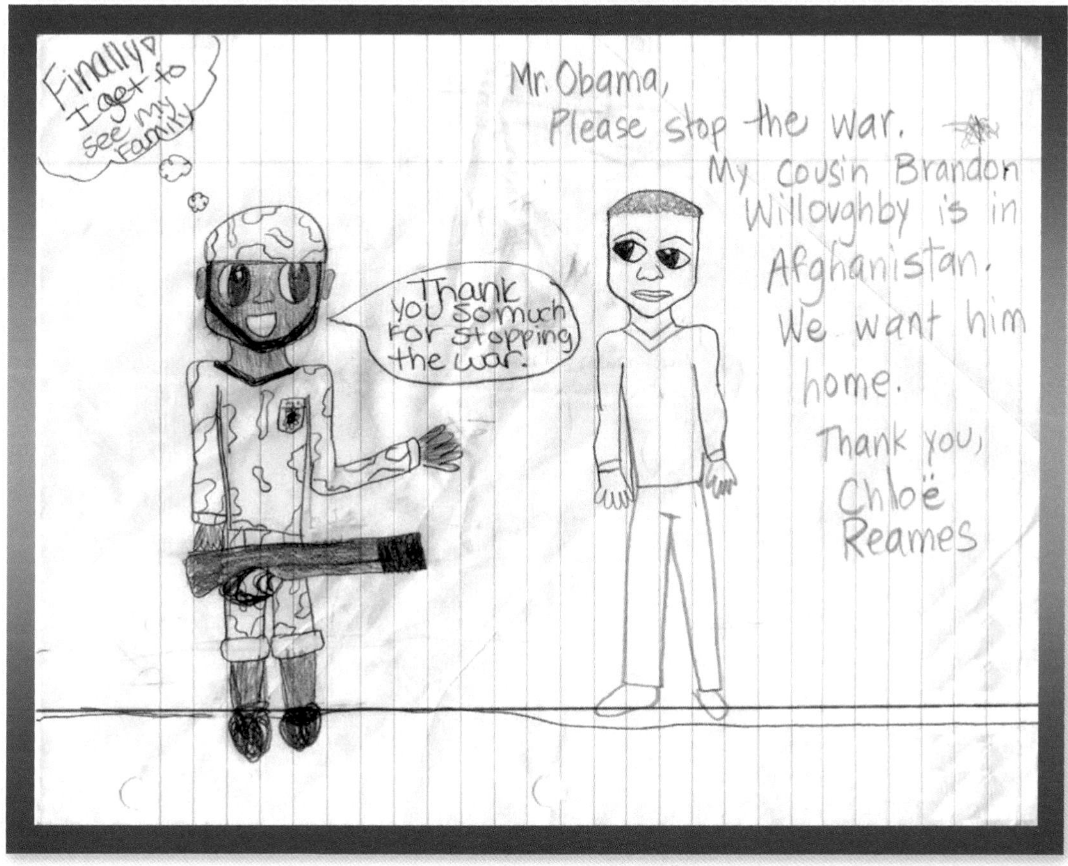

Mr. Obama,
Please stop the war.
My cousin Brandon Willoughby is in Afghanistan. We want him home.
Thank you,
Chloë Reames

CHLOË REAMES, 12, FLAGLER BEACH, FLORIDA

NAOMI GRANT

Dear Barack Obama,

America is the land of opportunity--and the land of change. I think it's definitely time for a new president.

President-elect Obama, you will take office at a difficult time in our nation's history. I think that, first and foremost, you need to fix the economy. This will make all of our lives easier, and it also might make it easier for you to bring the troops our of Iraq, which should have happened a long time ago.

Healthcare is also important. Like police officers and fire fighters, doctors should be paid by our taxes, not by our pocket money. Inexpensive healthcare is a much more important cause for our taxes to pay for, unlike building that new parking garage on that street over there.

All of the above will be difficult. But as you say, "Yes, we can!!!"

Naomi Grant

NAOMI GRANT, 11, LAWRENCE, KANSAS

Dear Mr. Obama,

I think that you shoud Power the white house With Solar or wind energy. I also think you should try to fix the economy. I think that you will be a great president.

From,
Carsten, age 9
Allen TX.

Dear Mr. Obama,

While you are President of the United States I think you should work on Powering stores with Wind energy. Good luck being President!,

From ainsley
age 7
Allen Tx

CARSTEN STADLER, 9, ALLEN, TEXAS

AINSLEY STADLER, 7, ALLEN, TEXAS

December 4, 2008

Mr. President-Elect Obama,

Congratulations on becoming the President. I realize you must be busy with global relations and the U.S. economic crisis, but I would like to inform you of of a national that is often overlooked. The oppression of and stereotypes toward skateboarders. We are often misunderstood ang categorized as vandals and delinquents, but that is far from the truth. Skateboarding is a positive form of self-expression, that actually has helped peope in under-privaloged areas away from drugs.

Skateboarding isn't a sport, it's a lifestyle. Its progression can't be stopped, only hindered or helped. Skateboarding gives us the ultimate sense of freedom and expression, but that feeling is often crushed by predjudiced laws. We ask your help now, as you are the only one who can change this. We can only do so much.

Sincerely,

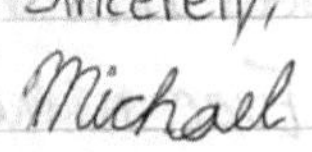

Michael

MICHAEL TALLEY, 13, URBANA, MARYLAND

Dear President Obama,

Hi, Mr. Obama. I'm Timothy Paul Smith. I live in Mansfield, Texas. Congratulations on being President of the United States of America. I want you to do these things to make our country special.

I want you to visit more states around the United States of America.

I want you to try to stop pollution.

Some of my friends and I will help you stops drugs and make sure people don't smoke or drink alcohol so that they can be very DRUG FREE.

If you want to ask me about something, just write a letter.

Sincerely,

Timothy Paul Smith

Timothy Paul Smith

TIMOTHY PAUL SMITH, 9, MANSFIELD, TEXAS

CAITLIN DILLON, 8, HAMILTON, MONTANA

Dear Obama January 2009

Our class voted for the presitant and John mcCain won. But you won the real election. I hope you help the world and make the environment a better place. I hope you try to make people stop littering. I hope you are a great presitant.

Caitlin Dillon
Hamilton MT.

KATJA

Dear President Obama,

I am so glad you were elected!

I was so concerned about the election that I postponed by birthday party (my birthday is October the 31st) because it would have been impossible for me to enjoy my birthday if you were not elected. (I had my birthday party yesterday, January 4th.)

To help get you elected, I canvassed door to door in Bucks County, PA, on five weekends, including my birthday weekend, with a grown-up (sometimes my mom and dad, but also other people) and talked to people about your policies and why you should be president. I think I changed a few people's minds and got them to vote for you.

Now that you are President, I want to tell you some of my ideas about health care. One thing I think you have to make sure of is that people, no matter how rich or poor, get equally good treatment. Also, it would be even better if we had a single-payer system. You should not have to depend on your job for health care, especially in this economic crisis, when many Americans don't have jobs and can't afford health care.

Thank you for reading my ideas. I am sure you can make America better.

Sincerely,

Katja Stroke-Adolphe, age 10

KATJA STROKE-ADOLPHE, 10, NEW YORK, NEW YORK

David Smith
Blue

Hi, my name is David Smith
And I live in Maryland.
Your presidency will be tough,
So I'll offer you a hand.

I give you this "to-do" list;
It will help you on your way.
In the shape of this here poem,
My hopes and dreams I'll say.

Our economy is failing;
It's not too hard to see.
Banks are dropping off our maps
And stocks aren't worth their fee.

The environment is next on my list
And I just may have a solution.
Alternative energy is the key;
It'll help get rid of the pollution.

Other countries can help us out,
So improve our foreign policy.
If they would just help our cause,
That would be good enough for me.

I have one last request of you
For my list is nearly over.
My three requests are written here
Like three leaves on a clover.

So plant my clover of hopes and dreams
As I give you all my best wishes.
Listen to America's people
And give my regards to the Mrs.

DAVID L. SMITH, 14, IJAMSVILLE, MARYLAND

RACHEL COVEY, 10, NEW YORK, NEW YORK

Dear President Obama,
Congratulations on becoming president! I have a few suggestions for you.

① I think anyone who presently workes at an animal shelter or who has ever worked at one <u>or</u> who has adopted an animal from one should get a tax break.

② I think you should stop animals geting put to sleep. (Maybe instead you can adopt them yourself and let them live in the White House?)

③ I really believe that a good percent of our taxes should go to a "greener" environment and hybrid cars should be more popular.

I believe in you,
Sincerely,

Rachel Covey

Dear president Obama
please don't raise taxes too much.
It is very expensive to live in new york city and my dad works very hard.

Also tell the car companies to make more hybrid sports cars.
Good luck !!!!

Sincerely Evan Covey

P.S I love sports cars.

P.P.S I hope the new president car you got is a hybrid.

EVAN COVEY, 7, NEW YORK, NEW YORK

NYIR KUEK, 9, LINCOLN, NEBRASKA

"There is not
a black America
and a white
America and a
Latino America
and an Asian
America.
There's the
United States
of America."
—Barack Obama

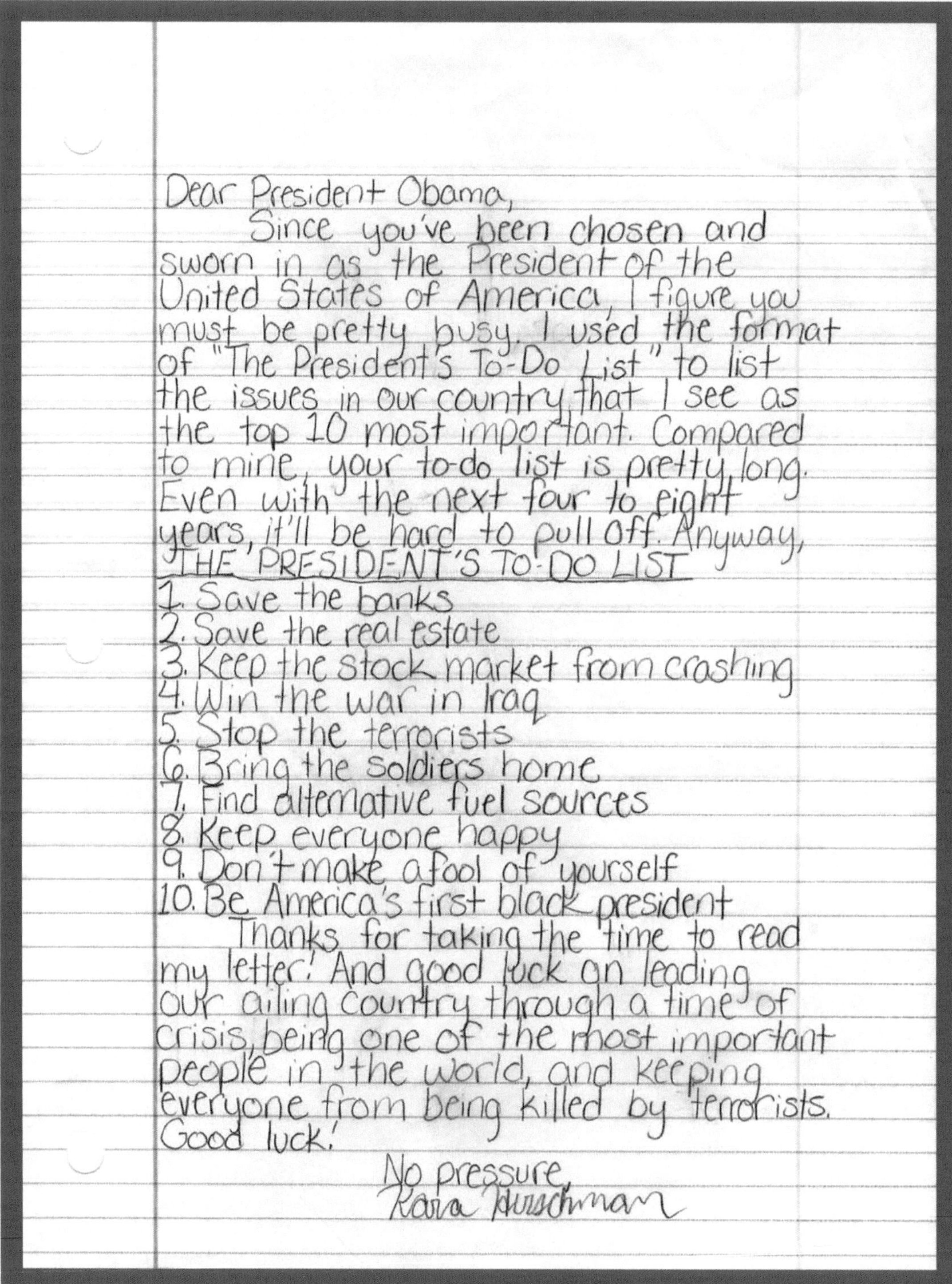

Dear President Obama,

Since you've been chosen and sworn in as the President of the United States of America, I figure you must be pretty busy. I used the format of "The President's To-Do List" to list the issues in our country that I see as the top 10 most important. Compared to mine, your to-do list is pretty long. Even with the next four to eight years, it'll be hard to pull off. Anyway,

THE PRESIDENT'S TO-DO LIST

1. Save the banks
2. Save the real estate
3. Keep the stock market from crashing
4. Win the war in Iraq
5. Stop the terrorists
6. Bring the soldiers home
7. Find alternative fuel sources
8. Keep everyone happy
9. Don't make a fool of yourself
10. Be America's first black president

Thanks for taking the time to read my letter! And good luck on leading our ailing country through a time of crisis, being one of the most important people in the world, and keeping everyone from being killed by terrorists. Good luck!

No pressure,
Kara Hirschman

KARA HIRSCHMAN, 12, IJAMSVILLE, MARYLAND

PAOLA WERNICK, 10, NEW YORK, NEW YORK

Dear President Obama,

I feel we should do something about global warming. I know it's nice to have natural heat, but soon enough, the world will over-heat. I want my kids-kids to see polar bears. I want them to see icebergs, which are melting incredibly fast. There are so many unneeded fuels and gases floating around in the air. We are consuming just too much each day. We should make eco-friendly cars, or ones that run on waste. As you said throughout your whole campaign, "We need Change."

— and we need it now.

Sincerely,
Paola Wernick

P.S. Is the White House eco-friendly?

Dear President obama, I think there are too many people throwing garbage in the ocean and on the street. And we need to stop that. So we need your help.

Sincerely,
Luca wernick age 7

LUCA WERNICK, 7, NEW YORK, NEW YORK

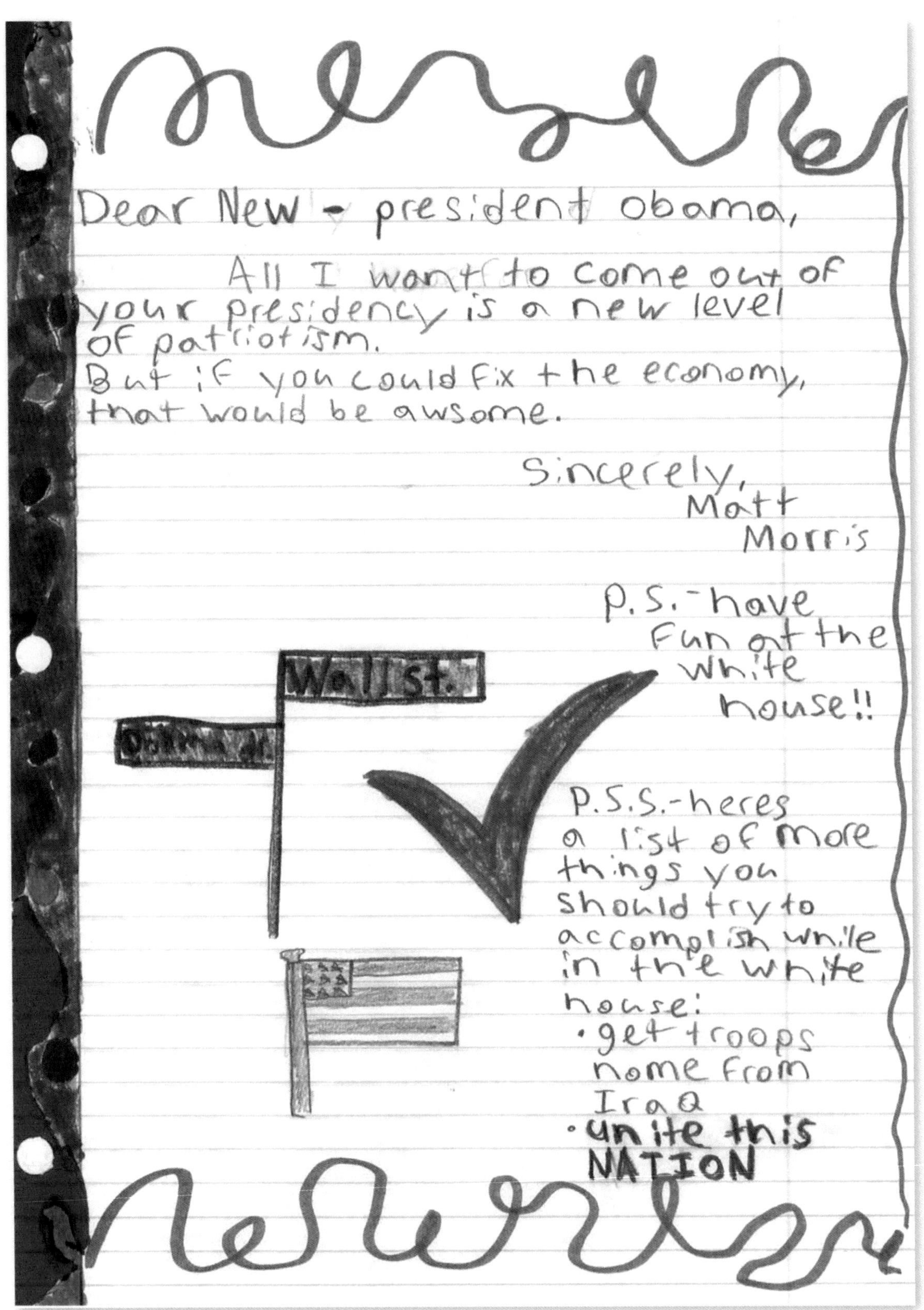
Dear New - president obama,

All I want to come out of your presidency is a new level of patriotism.
But if you could fix the economy, that would be awsome.

Sincerely,
Matt Morris

P.S. - have fun at the white house!!

P.S.S. - heres a list of more things you should try to accomplish while in the white house:
- get troops home from Iraq
- unite this NATION

MATTHEW MORRIS, 13, FREDERICK, MARYLAND

TARA PAGANO-TOUB, 10, NEW YORK, NEW YORK

Dear President Barack Obama,

I am very excited that you won! I went canvassing, sold buttons and handed out flyers for your campaign. At school I studied a lot about the election but the reason I am writing to you is to ask you what you are going to do about global warming and how are you going to fix schools? Are you going to bring the troops out of Iraq?. I hope you do.

Yes we can! Yes we can!

Tara Pagano-Toub
Age: 10

From ELLIE (as dictated to her Mom)

Dear Barack Obama,

I really want to meet you. I wish I could see you in person but I'm writing this letter to ask you what your job is. I'm learning Spanish at school and I can even say a poem in Spanish. My school is teaching me in dual-language. Do you speak Spanish?

How old are your kids? I'm 6 years old. My name is Eleanor Suzanne Adams. Everyone calls me Ellie.

I hope to see you soon.

From Ellie

P.S. Are you coming to Dallas?

ELLIE ADAMS, 6, DALLAS, TEXAS

Nov. 29, 2008

Dear Mr. Obama,

My name is Eleanor Heinrich, and I am 13 years old. Someday when I have kids who are born in America, it is my hope that they will see a better America when they first open their eyes, and later when they ask how and why our country has grown and developed into such a great nation, I believe that I can reply to those children in the future: There are many moments that defined change, and many reasons why change existed, but if you ask me, the first spark, the first speck of light, was on November the third, 2008, when all throughout Grant Park and all throughout the country, and even all throughout the whole world, rang the words, yes we can.

And to my children and the rest of the children of the future, I can say that my voice was joined with those millions of others, even if I couldn't hear them. Yes, I know we can.

Best wishes,
Eleanor Heinrich

P.S. Golden retrievers make great family dogs, if Sasha + Malia are wondering ☺

ELEANOR HEINRICH, 13, DWIGHT, ILLINOIS

Dear Mr. Obama

Thank you for thinking about our country first. I'm so glad That you won. And hearing about what you are going to do when you're president/what I heard in your Speeches. Oh and happy holidays. I hope you have a good time in the whithose. My family, Nolan, Wyatt, Ruby, and me hope you and your family have fun. I hope you Support the Country with respect.

Love, your ★
friend Vreeland

P.S. I'm 8 years old. and I want to change the world. How can I?

VREELAND TOBIN, 8, MONTCLAIR, NEW JERSEY

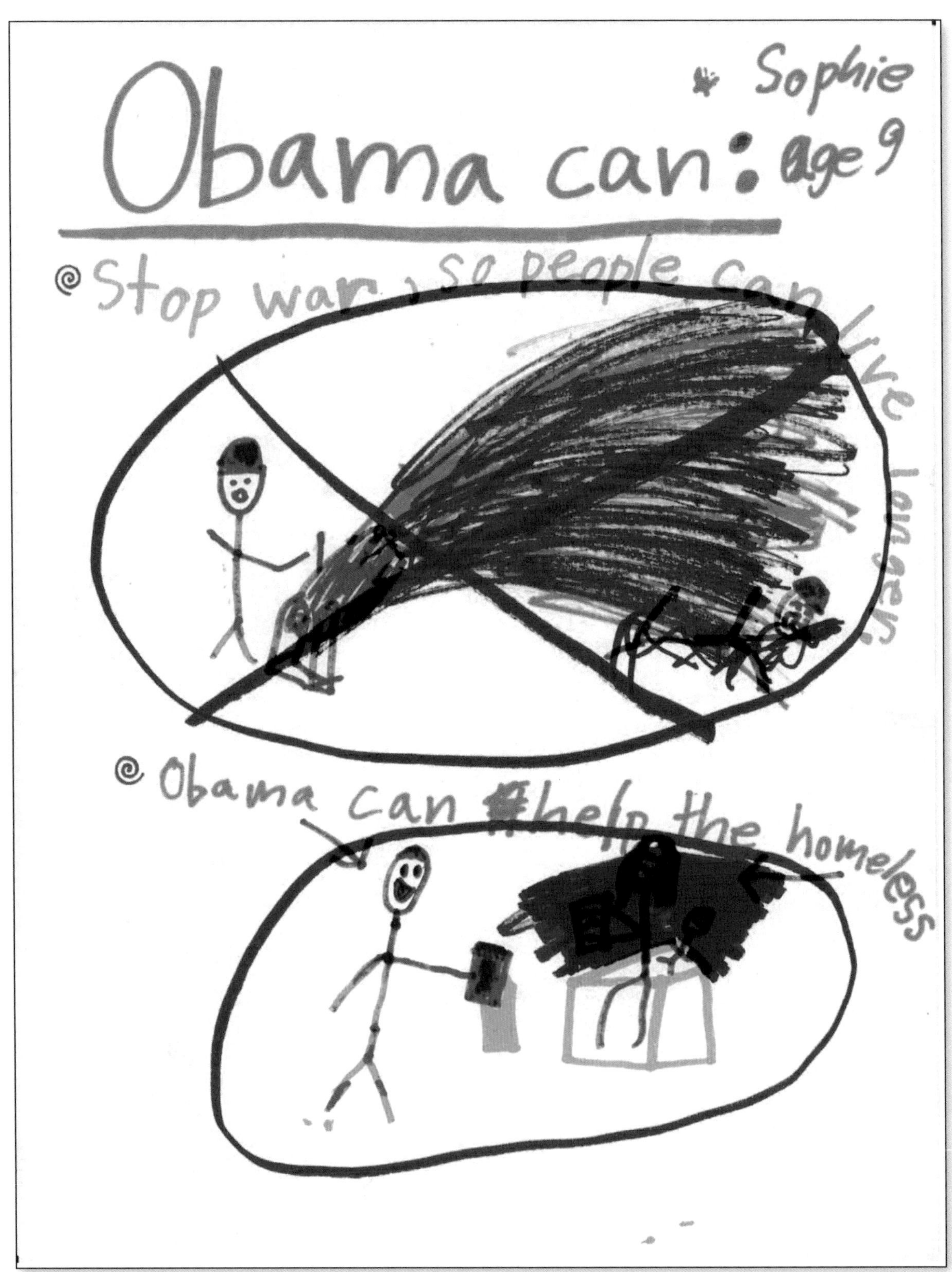

SOPHIE MILLAR, 9, NEW YORK, NEW YORK

<u>Now</u>

Jefferson Choi

Now you are the president.
Now you make our decision.
Now you made world history.
Now you can change U.S.
Now we pray.
Now we give peace.
Now we stand.
Now we wait.
Now the U.S will change.
Now the citizens are pleased.
Now the U.S is in a crisis.
Now the world is changing.
Now bring the troops back to our home, the beautiful.
Now recover the homeless.
Now save the endangered.
Now show us what you're made of.
This is now.
Then was then.
You can change this all now.
President Barack Obama is now.

JEFFERSON CHOI, 13, FREDERICK, MARYLAND

from Rebecca

Dear President-Elect Barack Obama,

You are an inspiration not only to me, but to this country. You have broken barriers that have stood tall for what seems like an eternity. When you speak to us, your strength shines through like rays of light beaming among all those who stand before you. You have given me hope for the future that this country will continue to stand strong and be able to overcome its battles to achieve greatness.

I cannot help but be honored when I say that you are our nation's first black president. It is not only an outstanding accomplishment but a great stride for this country. I believed in you from day one, and you have proven to me that anything is possible. Although I was not old enough to vote, you had such an impact on me that I knew in my heart that I had to do what I could to raise awareness about your campaign. Volunteering for the campaign for change was one of my proudest moments because I was fighting for a cause that I believed in.

No matter what age, race or gender, you represent all people who would stand by you, no matter what. You have allowed me to see that there is always a time and place for change—and that time is now. You are a brave and honorable man to step up and lead this country through one of its worst times. The beginning of the Declaration Of Independence states, "We hold these truths to be self-evident, that all men are created equal, that they are endowed by their Creator with certain unalienable Rights, that among these are Life, Liberty, and the Pursuit of Happiness." I now can say that there is truth behind the phrase that all men are created equal.

On the evening of November 4th, 2008 tears of joy fell from the eyes of happy citizens from coast to coast. Because of what you were able to do, lives were lifted and people rejoiced. You lifted a weight that rested upon so many shoulders and that is why there is so much love and appreciation sent your way. Americans united in their volunteer efforts, which shows what you had already done and—you weren't even president yet! To be able to bring so many people together for one cause is beyond amazing and I commend you for being such a wonderful role model. Children and adults look up to you, which is not easy to do. You have changed my life for the better and I thank you for that.

Barack Obama, you are a hero to the United States of America. Barack Obama, you are my hero.

Sincerely,
Rebecca Atkins

REBECCA ATKINS, 17, SANDIA PARK, NEW MEXICO

Dear President Obama,
Help us be nice.
Get everyone in the circle,
and then you can tell them
to listen to you.

Love,

Rukiya

RUKIYA HOLLAND-THOMAS, 5, MONTCLAIR, NEW JERSEY

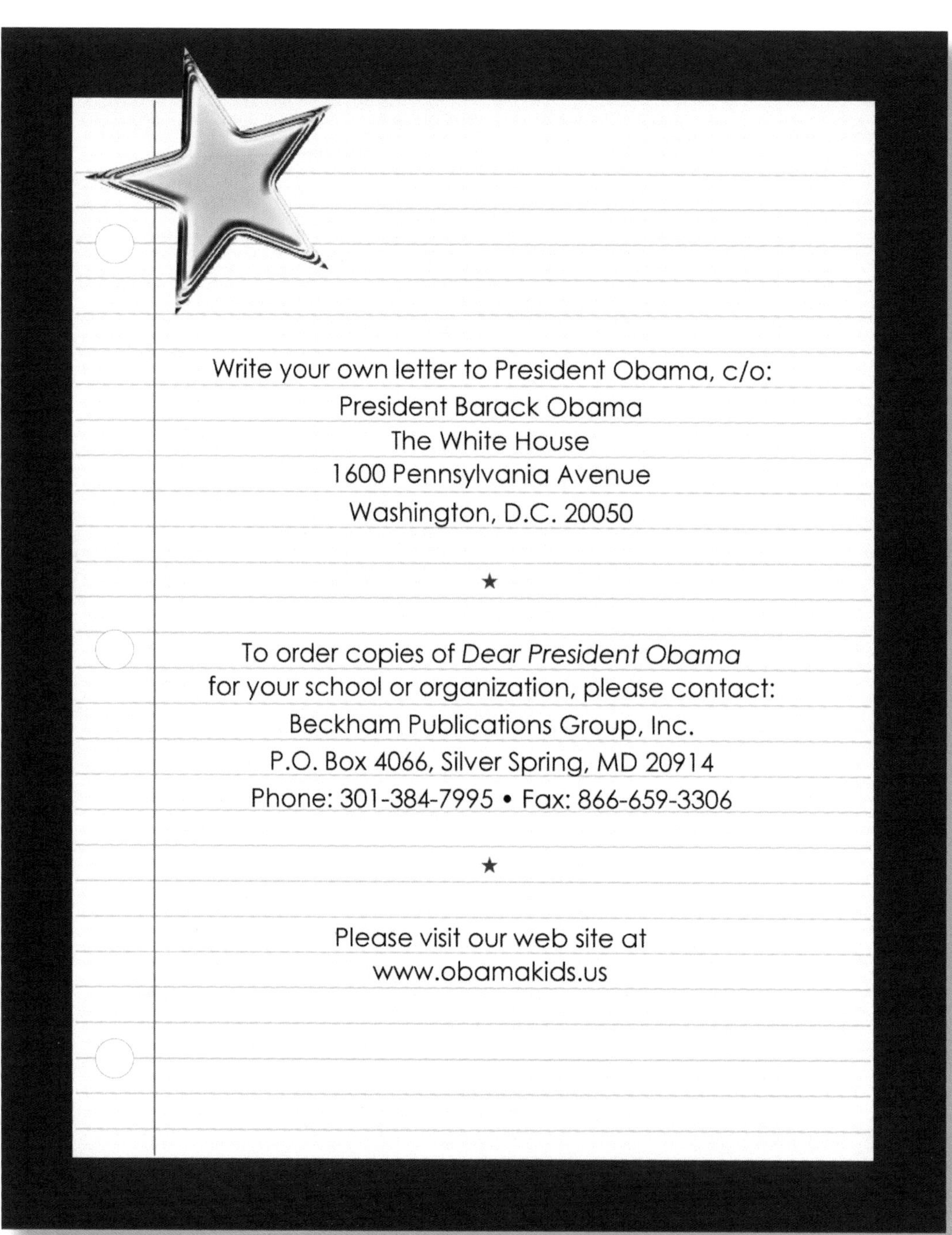

Write your own letter to President Obama, c/o:
President Barack Obama
The White House
1600 Pennsylvania Avenue
Washington, D.C. 20050

★

To order copies of *Dear President Obama*
for your school or organization, please contact:
Beckham Publications Group, Inc.
P.O. Box 4066, Silver Spring, MD 20914
Phone: 301-384-7995 • Fax: 866-659-3306

★

Please visit our web site at
www.obamakids.us

ABOUT THE EDITORS

BRUCE KLUGER (www.brucekluger.com) is a writer, columnist and commentator whose work appears nationwide in newspapers and magazines and on the Internet. A member of the Board of Contributors of *USA Today*, Bruce is also a Contributing Editor of *Parenting* magazine, and a regular contributor to National Public Radio, *The Los Angeles Times*, and *The Huffington Post*. He has written about current events, family and the popular culture for, among others, *The New York Times*, *The Chicago Tribune*, *The Baltimore Sun*, *The Boston Globe*, *Newsweek*, Time.com, Salon.com, Alternet.org, NickJr.com and the Sesame Street Workshop. He co-edited the books *The Right Words at the Right Time, Vol. 2: Your Turn!* (Atria Books) and *Thanks & Giving: All Year Long* (Simon and Schuster Children's Publishing), by Marlo Thomas. (The CD version of the latter book, for which Bruce served as Associate Producer, won the 2006 Grammy Award for Best Spoken Word Album for Children.) Since 2001, Bruce has written satire with David Slavin. Their work is regularly featured on NPR's *All Things Considered* and in *The Los Angeles Times*. Their satirical memoir, *Young Dick Cheney: Great American* (AlterNet Books), was published in April 2008. Bruce lives in Manhattan with his wife and two daughters.

DAVID TABATSKY (www.tabatsky.com) is the co-author of *Chicken Soup for the Soul: The Cancer Book (101 Stories of Courage, Support & Love)*. He was Consulting Editor for Marlo Thomas's bestselling collection, *The Right Words at the Right Time, Volume 2: Your Turn* (Atria Books). David wrote and published two editions of *What's Cool Berlin*, a comic travel guide to Germany's capital, and has written about family and culture for, among others, *The Forward*, *Parenting* magazine, and *Sesame Street Parent*. He has worked professionally in theatre and circus as an actor, clown and juggler, appearing at New York's Lincoln Center, Radio City Music Hall and Beacon Theatre, as well as throughout United States, Europe, Russia and Japan (including his critically acclaimed solo performance at the Edinburgh Fringe Festival). David has taught and directed for The American School of London, die Etage in Berlin, the Big Apple Circus School and the United Nations International School. He is on the theatre faculty at Adelphi University and is a teaching artist for The Henry Street Settlement. David lives in New York City with his children, Max and Stella.

Printed in the United States
149379LV00005B